"Full of wise, playful, and effective strategies…if every parent picked up this book, we'd have a lot happier families."

—**Elisha Goldstein, PhD**, cofounder of the Center for Mindful Living and author of *Uncovering Happiness*

"This book is a great introduction to mindfulness, and it has a wealth of simple but effective practices that parents can do with their children. Carla shows us how to help our kids pay attention, regulate their emotions, develop empathy, and ultimately understand themselves. Carla's writing is honest, relatable, and funny—this book will be a blessing for parents (and their kids)!"

—**Sarah Rudell Beach, MEd**, mindfulness instructor, executive director of Brilliant Mindfulness, LLC, and creator of the website leftbrainbuddha.com

"Carla Naumburg always keeps it real—with wisdom, humor, humility, and profound compassion. In *Ready, Set, Breathe*, she offers simple, practical tools for parents and kids to be more mindful, starting today."

—**Deborah Sosin, LICSW, MFA**, author of *Charlotte and the Quiet Place*

"*Ready, Set, Breathe* fulfills on its promise, providing simple, doable practices to support parents in bringing mindfulness into the sweet chaos of family life. The writing is honest and engaging, with healthy doses of the humor and compassion all parents need."

—**Amy Saltzman, MD**, author *A Still Quiet Place*

"Multitasking parents can take more than a page from this simple, sweet, and straightforward guide to mindfully preventing meltdowns not just in our kids, but in ourselves as well."

—**Christopher Willard, PsyD**, Harvard Medical School, author of *Growing Up Mindful* and other books

"Clear, thoughtful, and funny. This wonderful and candid book gives us ways to bring the miracle of mindfulness to our families. For all the parents out there who have been wondering how to bring mindfulness to their children, Carla has written the comprehensive guide. I will be recommending and referencing this book for a long time to come! Carla gives so many simple and varied ways to share mindfulness and have more peaceful families. Plus, she's the clearest, most down-to-earth writer about mindfulness that I've ever read (and I've read many). A book that may change your life!"

—**Hunter Clarke-Fields, MSAE, RYT**, founder of Hunter Yoga

"This book gives parents a wealth of tools, activities, and explorations that can make parenting more joyful and engaging, while supporting the well-being of the entire family. Carla shares these ideas in a loving, humor-filled, realistic way that will immediately put you at ease—you'll feel like you're talking with a good friend."

—**Jennifer Cohen Harper, MA, E-RCYT**, founder of Little Flower Yoga and the School Yoga Project, author of *Little Flower Yoga for Kids*, and mom of Isabelle May

"Carla Naumburg's book *Ready, Set, Breathe* is a wonderfully engaging and easy-to-understand gift to parents, offering simple yet meaningful ways to practice mindfulness themselves and with their children."

—**Susan Kaiser Greenland**, author of *The Mindful Child* and cofounder of Inner Kids

ready, set, breathe

Practicing Mindfulness with Your Children for Fewer Meltdowns and a More Peaceful Family

CARLA NAUMBURG, PhD

New Harbinger Publications, Inc.

Publisher's Note

This publication is designed to provide accurate and authoritative information in regard to the subject matter covered. It is sold with the understanding that the publisher is not engaged in rendering psychological, financial, legal, or other professional services. If expert assistance or counseling is needed, the services of a competent professional should be sought.

Distributed in Canada by Raincoast Books

New Harbinger Publications, Inc.
5674 Shattuck Avenue
Oakland, CA 94609
www.newharbinger.com

Cover design by Sara Christian
Acquired by Melissa Valentine
Edited by Brady Kahn

Library of Congress Cataloging-in-Publication Data

Naumburg, Carla.
Ready, set, breathe : practicing mindfulness with your children for fewer meltdowns and a more peaceful family / Carla Naumburg.
pages cm
Includes bibliographical references.
ISBN 978-1-62625-290-5 (paperback) -- ISBN 978-1-62625-291-2 (pdf e-book) -- ISBN 978-1-62625-292-9 (epub) 1. Parenting--Psychological aspects. 2. Stress management. 3. Games--Psychological aspects. 4. Parent and child. I. Title.
HQ755.8.N387 2015
306.874--dc23

2015030062

Printed in the United States of America

20 19 18

10 9 8 7 6 5 4 3 2

This book is dedicated to my village—to all of my parent friends out there who are also struggling to raise their children with as much kindness and skill as possible. Parenting isn't an easy journey, and I am so grateful to be traveling it alongside all of you. Thank you for your humor, your honesty, and your support. My life with two little ones wouldn't be half as much as fun without all of you.

Contents

Introduction

"Will you *please* just *calm down* and *take a breath*?" I snapped at my five-year-old daughter the other morning. We had both gotten up on the wrong side of the bed, and things had gone downhill from there. She was circling me in the kitchen, whining and crying because we had run out of her favorite cereal and I had denied her request to take a tiny and very beloved toy to preschool. Her four-year-old sister, who was supposed to be sitting at the table eating her breakfast, kept getting down to grab a toy or to finish a drawing she was working on, and I had to keep reminding her to get back in her seat and finish eating. Meanwhile, I was stressed about everything that I needed to do that morning: make lunches, get dressed, finish packing my work bags, and hustle everyone out the door on time. In the back of my mind, I was feeling guilty about leaving that afternoon for a three-day work trip. Even though I knew that the girls would be fine at home with their dad, I also knew that my impending absence was part of why my daughter was having such a hard morning, and I couldn't help but feel bad about it. Not unlike my little girl, I was tired and overwhelmed, and barking at her to breathe was the closest I could get to my mindfulness practice in that moment—which is to say, not very close at all.

Not surprisingly, she responded in kind. "I don't want to breathe, Mommy!"

The ridiculousness of her statement may have been lost on her, but it snapped me out of my own irritability just long enough to give me a little perspective. I put down the peanut butter knife, put my hands flat on the counter, and took a few deep breaths. When I felt myself calm down a little bit, I picked up my daughter, sat down with her on my lap, and kept breathing. Eventually her heaving chest calmed down and her breathing became more slow and steady. After a few minutes, she asked me what I was doing.

"I'm just breathing. That's all."

"Oh," she replied with a smile. "Me too!"

And so we sat for a few minutes and just breathed together. While I know that she actually was breathing, I don't know if she was aware of her breath in the same way that I was. I had been purposefully paying attention to the air moving in and out of my nose, and each time a stressful thought entered my mind about everything I had to get done or how I was going to get her sister to eat her breakfast, I let the thought go and came back to my breath. For all I know, my daughter could have been thinking about baby dolls or unicorns or ice cream sandwiches—anything but her breathing. The truth is that it doesn't really matter. By the time I went back into the kitchen, we were both feeling a lot calmer, more connected, and present with each other and with ourselves. It's not that anything had really changed: my daughter still wasn't getting her favorite breakfast or bringing her toy to school, and I still had a million things to do. The difference was that once we had calmed down, rather than freaking out in our own minds and subsequently all over each other, we were both able to deal with these challenges a little more effectively.

The moment that set our morning on a better path was the moment when I put down the knife and took a few deep breaths. When I did that, I was intentionally trying to get myself into a more *mindful mind-set*, which is simply about paying attention to whatever is happening, right here and right now, without judging it or wishing it were different. I had spent most of the morning doing one thing with my body—showering, getting dressed, or making breakfast—and another thing with my mind, generally stressing, worrying, and feeling guilty. This split attention characterizes the way most of us move through our daily lives most of the time, often without even noticing it. Multitasking often feels unavoidable in modern life, and it can, at times, help us be a bit more efficient. More often than not, however, it leads to increased stress, mistakes and errors, and snappy responses to our children. When I was in the kitchen making sandwiches, I was so wrapped up in my own unhelpful thoughts that I wasn't really paying attention to what was going on with my daughter, which is how we got caught up in a power struggle over toys and cereal. But after taking the time to notice what was really happening, I was able to respond to it in a much more skillful and effective way: by giving my daughter the attention she had been asking for all along. The deep breaths I took were an important step in helping me get out of my own head and back into the present, and that's what mindful parenting is all about: making a choice to focus our attention on the present moment, with kindness and curiosity, so we can make a thoughtful choice about how to proceed rather than react out of frustration or confusion.

We adults aren't the only ones who get distracted by our own thoughts, are stressed out by things we can't control, and find it hard to manage our big feelings well. Our children struggle with these issues as well, and they need our help in learning how to deal with these challenges in effective, empathic ways. Many of us turn to star charts and time-outs, and those can be useful, up to a point. The problem is that those are external sources of feedback and discipline, and if we parents aren't there, neither is the behavior change. Mindfulness, which is based on our internal experience and perspective, is a skill that our children can always carry with them, no matter what else is going on. This will be covered in more detail in chapter 1, but first it will be helpful to have a better sense of what our children struggle with and why.

Understanding Our Children's Struggles

On that morning, like so many other mornings, my daughters were struggling with three of the most common challenges that young children face on a daily basis: stress, emotional regulation, and attentional difficulties. These are part of the human experience and something that every child deals with to some extent and for a variety of different reasons. First, much of what kids face every day, from schoolwork to bullies to that green blob on their dinner plate, can, and does, feel stressful, scary, and completely beyond their control—because it often is. Furthermore, learning how to deal with life's challenges and difficult feelings in healthy, productive ways is part of their developmental work. Our children are still figuring out how to identify and label their feelings as well as how to respond to them, which is why they throw toys and tantrums when they're frustrated. Finally, their brains, and specifically the parts responsible for relatively advanced skills such as calming down, paying attention, and making good choices, aren't yet fully developed, which means the part of their brain that likes to fight, flee, freeze, or freak out is more likely to step in when things get bumpy. As you will learn throughout this book, mindfulness practice can help children deal more effectively with stress, emotional regulation, and attentional difficulties.

Stress

If you were to ask most folks to define stress, they would probably talk about having too much work to do, or struggling to navigate a challenging situation or deal with a difficult person. It often feels as though if the rest of the world—our bosses or our parents or our children's teachers, or whoever—would just calm down, our stress levels would go down. The problem with that perspective is that it doesn't acknowledge the role that we each play in our own perception of and response to stress. Everyone responds differently to difficult situations depending on their temperament, style, life experience, support, and coping skills, among other things. I like the definition of stress often attributed to the psychologist Richard Lazarus (1966), which focuses on our relationship to what is happening in our lives and our sense of whether or not we can handle it. When we feel like we can't handle what's happening, regardless of what it is, we get stressed.

There are some situations that are likely to be universally stressful for children, ranging from divorce, loss and illness, bullying, and academic difficulties to homelessness, neglect, or abuse. However, it's important to keep in mind that any number of life situations, including those that we may write off as normal childhood challenges, such as starting a new school, overscheduled days, fighting with a brother or sister, watching a scary movie, having a disagreement on the playground, or saying goodbye to a parent heading out on a work trip, can be frequent sources of stress in a child's life. While some amount of stress is useful for children, as it may motivate them to do their homework, clean up their rooms, or score the game-winning goal on the soccer field, too much stress can have a damaging impact on their bodily functioning, brain development, and ability to learn and integrate new information. Stress builds up over time, and even small stressors that aren't released or managed can impact children in significant ways. Children who are experiencing high levels of stress may have difficulties sleeping, eating, paying attention, thinking clearly, solving problems, playing well with friends, and behaving well at home and at school.

Emotional Regulation

Let's say you head out to your favorite restaurant for dinner only to learn that they no longer serve the pasta dish that you had been thinking about all week. How would you respond? My guess is that you'd feel bummed, and you might even say something to the waiter about how much you'd like to see that dish back on the menu, but then you'd order something else. I suspect you probably wouldn't lie down on the floor and start screaming madly until someone picked you up and carried you outside. The reason you wouldn't have a toddler-style tantrum is because you have developed the ability to regulate your emotions. You would allow yourself to express some concern about the menu change, so you could feel heard, but you would also be able to remember that screaming in restaurants isn't a socially acceptable behavior, so you wouldn't do it, as much as you might want to.

Emotional regulation, or the ability to not immediately act out in response to every feeling that we experience, is one of the biggest challenges that many children face. When kids are dysregulated, they tend to scream, hit, bite, throw things, or engage in other problematic behaviors. They may have a hard time calming down. Not unlike stress reactions, the ability to recognize and manage emotions will vary greatly from child to child. We all know some kids who seem quite good at getting and staying calm, while others quite simply aren't. Children who have a hard time managing difficult or uncomfortable feelings may struggle academically and socially; if they can't tolerate the boredom of a math test, they're unlikely to finish it. If they throw a tantrum or a bat on the playground or the sports field, they're unlikely to develop and sustain friendships.

While some amount of difficulty managing big feelings is part of the normal developmental process (no one expects an infant to be able to wait patiently for her next meal when she's feeling hungry), there are ways of interacting with and responding to our children that may help them avoid the meltdown or at least help them settle down as soon as possible when it happens. I'll talk more about this throughout the book, but here's the short version: get yourself calm, connect with your child's experience, help her identify and label what she's feeling, and from there you can help her get present and grounded.

Attentional Difficulties

According to the US Centers for Disease Control and Prevention (2014), more and more children are being diagnosed with attention deficit/hyperactivity disorder, or ADHD, each year. Everyone seems to have a different theory to explain this trend, from doctors getting better at identifying symptoms to chemicals in the water we're drinking. The reality is that no one knows for sure what's going on, but we do know this: nothing about our daily lives encourages children to pay attention for any extended period of time. We rush our kids through their days, shepherding them quickly from one activity to the next. They stare at screens with brightly colored images that change every few seconds, or they click around from one website to the next, never fully considering the information on each one.

Modern society isn't the only challenge to our children's ability to keep their attention focused on just one thing. It's also part of human nature. Our brains were made to think, wonder, worry, question, remember, speculate, and guess about pretty much anything and everything. Our minds are designed to constantly scan the environment. Sometimes this can be quite useful, such as when a young soccer player is able to notice a big hole in the middle of the field and run around it on her way to the goal. Being able to switch their attention quickly from one thing to another can be useful for children, as long as they are able to pay attention to just one thing when they want or need to. Problems arise when they aren't capable of choosing what to focus on but are instead randomly distracted by any shiny object or random thought that happens to cross their path.

When that happens, we tell our kids to "Pay attention!" or "Focus!" However, if we never clearly describe to them what focusing is and how to do it and never give them opportunities to practice, it's unlikely they'll ever get better at it. Teaching our children how to direct and sustain their attention in specific, intentional ways will help them manage their stress and difficult feelings, and that's what mindfulness is all about. Mindfulness, or the practice of choosing to pay attention to whatever is happening right here and right now, without judging it or wishing it were different, is rooted in ancient wisdom and supported by modern science, including images of the brain and how it changes in response to mindfulness practice.

Fortunately, mindfulness is something we can teach our children, and it's not just about breathing with them. It is a way of approaching every minute of our lives—the good ones and the rough ones. As a result, there are many ways to share mindfulness with our kids. I will focus on three different methods, each of which will be explored more fully in this book:

1. Modeling mindfulness for your child. As any parent knows, our little ones aren't always the most responsive to our instructions or suggestions, to put it mildly. In those moments when they're just not interested, the best we can do is to respond to whatever is going on with as much awareness, acceptance, and kindness as we can muster. Each time we are able to do this, we are modeling a mindful response to a difficult situation for them. This is a crucial idea that I will keep coming back to in this book.

2. Sharing a specific activity, book, or guided meditation with the purpose of teaching the language, concepts, and practices of mindfulness. Your child will learn the most from these moments if you are both feeling relatively calm and connected. You may choose to read a picture book about a mindful monkey or to color mandalas together, take a mindful walk and discuss your experience, or share a brief gratitude practice before dinner.

3. Offering your kid the skills and tools for responding mindfully and soothing herself when she is having a difficult moment, such as taking three mindful breaths, spending some time in the calm-down corner (more about this in chapter 4), or "getting outside to go inside." These interventions will be most effective if you practice them alongside your child, rather than just telling her to do it, at least initially.

Feel free to experiment with a range of different ways to teach mindfulness to your child. It won't take long to figure out what works well for you and your family, and before long, practicing mindfulness will become a natural part of your lives together.

The Power of Practicing Mindfulness at Home

There are several wonderful books out there about teaching mindfulness to children (I've listed many of them in the resources section). For the most part, the practices and activities in those books are based on the authors' experience teaching children in schools and clinics. I highly recommend such classes if you can find one in your area; my daughters loved the after-school mindfulness course for kids that they recently took. However, as any parent or teacher can tell you, the experience of teaching and learning with our own children at home is quite different. Children learning mindfulness at school are generally in a relatively calm place; teachers have set aside a period of time specifically for practice, and they've carefully planned fun and interesting activities. In addition, teachers are much less likely to get into power struggles with their students. Finally, the power of peer pressure cannot be underestimated. A child is unlikely to yell, "But I don't want to breathe!" and stomp off in a huff in the middle of an activity at school.

Alternately, we parents are most likely to bring up mindfulness practices when our kids are having a hard time—when they're grumpy or frustrated or angry or sad—which may make them less interested in whatever we have to offer, because they may feel as though we're not acknowledging their feelings or that we're trying to fix them. No one likes to feel that way. In addition, our attempts to help our kids can be complicated by power dynamics, sibling rivalry, our own fatigue or frustration, or whatever else is happening just then. All of this means that teaching mindfulness at home to your own child is very different from teaching it to someone else's children at school, which is why I've written this book specifically for parents. It's also why this book is based on the experiences of parents who are currently teaching their children these skills and ideas in their own homes. I've interviewed almost thirty mothers and fathers about how they understand mindfulness, how they practice it, how they share it with their children, and, most importantly, what's worked and what hasn't.

We parents are in a unique position to introduce our children to the power of mindfulness in ways that just aren't possible at school. We're with our kids in their best and worst moments, which is precisely when the most powerful experiences and transformations can take place. Moreover, our children are intent on learning from us, primarily through observation and imitation, which gives us the chance to teach them in the most meaningful and lasting ways. I'm talking about the small and frequent interactions and responses that come to characterize our children's lives as much as the air they breathe. Through their experience with us over time, the ability to get focused, grounded, and calm in difficult situations can become second nature to our kids.

As effective as mindfulness is, I don't want you to get discouraged if the practices don't seem to have an impact right away or if your kid doesn't seem interested in the activity you're suggesting. First, you can't measure success by how any one exercise goes; it's more useful to observe how your child is doing overall. Often we don't notice the effects of mindfulness in the moment, but our kids may seem calmer and less reactive over time. In addition, unlike some other interventions that we might use with our children, mindfulness isn't just something we can hand to someone else when we need them to get into a better head space. As we'll explore later, mindfulness isn't about helping our children to get and stay happy. It's about accepting whatever is happening, no matter what it is. Sometimes that means savoring a beautiful moment more fully, but it can also mean getting quite wet in the rain with our kids until the latest emotional storm passes. The good news is that calming down and feeling better are common and lovely side effects of just being with our kids without freaking out about their freak-out. But if we start from a place of wanting things to be different or wanting to fix our children, we're missing the point of mindfulness.

Finally, as any parent who has ever tried to sleep- or potty-train a child knows, sometimes you get lucky the first time, but more often than not you have to try a few different methods, styles, and tools before you hit the jackpot. The same is true for mindfulness. The most important thing we can do is start by paying attention to our children—who they are, what they're interested in, what's worked in the past, and how we can build on their strengths. For example, my older daughter is extremely sensitive to smells and tastes, so an exercise involving smelling different odors and trying to guess what each one is probably wouldn't be a great place to start with her. She does love her baby dolls, though, so showing her how to breathe by having her lie down with a doll on her tummy and watch it move up and down as she rocks it to sleep with her breath is a much better match for her. Then again, you never know what's going to work and when. As one mother I interviewed noted, "It's all about trusting the process." We are "planting the seeds of mindfulness," as Zen master Thich Nhat Hanh (2011) describes it. The more seeds we plant, the more likely that one, or many, of them will take root and sprout. Take the mother who described how her son didn't seem interested in the yoga videos she tried to do with him, but then a few days later saw him watching the DVD when he thought she wasn't looking.

A Few More Things to Consider

There are many ways I could have responded to my daughter that morning in our kitchen other than snapping at her: I could have put her in time-out, given her what she wanted, or reminded her that if she could get through the morning without a tantrum, she would get a star on her chart. I had done all of these things in the past with limited or no success. But on that morning, I was able to remember mindfulness, which is a fairly different approach to our children's challenges. I shared this story with you because it illustrates several important points that will be explored more fully in the course of this book.

First of all, mindfulness is a specific way of engaging with and addressing challenging emotions, including sadness, anger, stress, frustration, and boredom. It's not about fixing or managing our children or making their problems go away; again, it's about learning to see and accept whatever is happening for ourselves and for them right now, in this moment, without judging it or wishing it were different. Once we are able to do that, we can make a thoughtful and skillful choice about how to proceed. When my daughter first started freaking out that morning, I just wanted her to quit it, and I reacted by barking at her. When I was finally able to stop, calm myself down, and accept that she needed a little more attention from me, I could make a choice about how to respond to her, one that eventually helped both of us move forward with a better morning. Even though I didn't run out to buy her the right cereal or cancel my work trip, we were both able to get to a better place fairly quickly. This idea of practicing mindfulness by paying attention and accepting what is happening so that we can choose our response is a vastly different approach to difficult situations than what most of us are used to.

Please don't worry if this is the first time you've ever picked up a book about mindfulness and if you have no idea what I'm talking about. I'm going to explain everything, including what it is, why it works, and, most importantly, how to do it.

It's important to keep in mind that teaching mindfulness is not like teaching someone to ride a bike—there's no magic moment when everything suddenly clicks and our work is done. Again, it's an ongoing process of experimenting and planting the seeds of mindfulness, which calls on us to continually share the concepts and practices of mindful living with our children in the hope that over time, the ideas will take root and grow.

You can't make another person be mindful. Mindfulness is a state of mind, and it's something that only your child can control. Once our kids realize this, mindfulness becomes an incredibly empowering experience for them. The flip side of that is that it's entirely possible, and even likely, that you will go through some of these activities with your kid, and her brain will be in a million different places the entire time—anywhere but the here and now. That's okay. Hang in there and keep offering mindful opportunities.

It's also important to note that mindfulness and the related activities should never be a punishment. Insisting that children meditate or take a few deep breaths when they've done something wrong is the fastest way to make them run in the opposite direction, as you saw from my story at the beginning of this book.

Mindfulness practice can make a big difference in a short period of time. In an ideal world, we would all be mindful all the time, but the reality is that most of us aren't raising our children in a Zen monastery. Mindfulness is like a muscle; the more we use it, the stronger it gets. As we help our kids continue to strengthen those muscles, just a few mindful breaths can help them calm down, figure out what's going on and what they need, and then make a choice about what to do next. Most of the exercises and activities in this book can be done in just a few minutes, and what really matters is being as consistent as possible in using them. The key here is frequency and consistency. Your practice will be more effective if you make time every day for one or two brief exercises—as little as five or ten minutes a day—rather than do one long activity once a week.

It's also true that any time your child is focused on, and fully immersed in, doing just one thing, whether it's drawing, playing soccer, building a tower, or playing outside, she is being mindful. I will talk more about this in chapter 3, but the point here is that you don't have to force your little one into a cross-legged position on a meditation cushion in order to teach her mindfulness. She's already doing it on her own; she just needs some help understanding why these mindful times matter and how she can practice them in a more consistent, intentional way.

An important caveat: screen time is not mindful time. There's really no way around this one. As much as our children may seem calm or focused when they're watching TV or playing a game on the iPad, it's not mindfulness practice, and it's not teaching them how to intentionally guide and sustain their attention. When our kids are staring at a screen, they're generally not aware of what they're doing, thinking, or feeling, and they're not noticing or getting curious about their own experience. If you've ever thought that your kiddo looks like a baby zombie as soon as the show starts, you're not entirely wrong. The thoughtful, intentional part of her brain pretty much shuts down, and she's mindlessly responding to the flashing images in front of her. I'm not saying you should never let your kid have any screen time; that's a decision each family should make for themselves. I'm just saying it shouldn't be mistaken for mindfulness practice.

One final and crucially important point: in order to teach mindfulness to your child, you must start with yourself. In fact, if you do nothing else besides work on your own mindfulness practice, your child will benefit immensely from your increased attention and acceptance. Without fail, the parents I interviewed said that this was their most important piece of advice to other parents: it's just not possible to get our children to a mindful place if we're not already there or at least willing to travel in that direction with them. As you can see from my attempt to help my daughter calm down, you don't have to be perfect at this, but you do need to keep practicing on your own and with your child. It's not always easy, but as you will see, it's definitely worth it.

How to Use This Book

This book is divided into two parts. In the first part, you'll learn more about what mindfulness is, how it works, and why it works. This section will explore why it is so important for you to practice mindfulness on your own and alongside your child, and how you can share your practice with her. I'll describe a number of easy ways to do this.

The second part will explore a range of ways to integrate mindfulness into your family life at home. Chapter 3 will teach you to notice those times when you and your child are already present and engaged with whatever is happening inside and around you, and how to build on those experiences. This will set the stage for later chapters on how to talk about mindfulness and how to choose the right activities and tools, because your attempts to teach mindfulness will be most effective and relevant when you build on your family's existing strengths and interests. This may mean spending more time in nature, listening to music together, playing games, cooking together, or practicing your religious or spiritual rituals. The fact is that you can do anything mindfully as long as you, well, put your mind to it. I have included over a hundred different activities, games, and tools in this book, most of which are based on interviews with parents who are using them. Every family has different styles and preferences, and what's important is to find something that makes sense for you and your child, so please feel free to modify anything in this book or create new practices. It all starts with paying attention and staying open. Once you do that, the creative ideas will follow, I promise.

I've included practices to try in every chapter of this book, so you can get started right away. Almost every activity is something you can do alongside your child, which again I strongly recommend doing. There will be some practices that your kid may prefer to do on her own, but, in general, she will likely be more receptive to whatever you are offering if you take the time to do it with her. I have a few additional tips for how to get the most from this book.

Enlist Your Child's Help

Whenever possible, enlist your child's help. If you get her involved in creating, choosing, and implementing mindfulness exercises, she will take more ownership over the experience and may come up with creative ideas you never would have thought of. One mother I spoke to noticed that her son was eating so quickly during meals that it was impacting her own ability to slow down, eat mindfully, and enjoy her food. She asked her son for suggestions as to how to change the dinnertime dynamic, and he suggested using a meditation app on her iPhone to set a timer for a two-minute silent meditation before each meal. Although her son knew she meditated, she had never directly taught him to do it, and yet he came up with this idea on his own. Now the whole family sits quietly together before dinner each night, and even though the kids don't necessarily meditate during those two minutes, the meals tend to be calmer and everyone eats a little more slowly.

Notice Your Feelings as You Read

As you read about the activities and exercises in this book, pay attention to how you are feeling. If you notice yourself getting interested in something or if it sparks an idea for you, make a note in the book and give it a try. If something seems cheesy, contrived, or just plain weird, then it might not be the right exercise for you and your family. One of the reasons I interviewed so many parents is because I know that every family is different, and what works for my husband, my daughters, and me might not work for anyone else, and vice versa. There are plenty of options in this book from which to pick and choose. Once you get in the habit of infusing your daily life with mindful moments, you'll find yourself coming up with new ways to help your child get and stay focused, present, and calm.

Engage Your Partner If Possible

It's great if your parenting partner is on board with introducing mindfulness. If so, I encourage you both to read this book and discuss how you can implement some of the ideas and practices I suggest. If your partner isn't interested, that's okay too. As mindfulness is about the intention and attention we bring to whatever we are doing, it's an excellent foundation for any parenting style, which means that you don't have to change everything you were doing before you started reading this book. You can keep doing all of those things with a little more thoughtfulness, awareness, and kindness. Your child will just learn that different people have different ways of managing situations, which is a great insight to have.

Choose the Right Tool for Your Child

This book is intended for parents of children between the ages of three and ten. From time to time, I will make suggestions about the age-appropriateness of certain activities, but in general, I will leave that decision up to you, the parent, for a couple reasons. One is that our children develop at vastly different rates and have widely varying interests. The other is that people, children and adults alike, may revert to younger behaviors when they're feeling stressed or upset or just in need of a break. My daughters and I enjoy sitting together and drawing pictures, and when we're paying full attention to what we're doing and being curious about what we're drawing, the different colors we're using, and the different ways to hold our markers to create thick or thin lines, it's absolutely a mindfulness practice. While coloring may be an age-appropriate activity for little girls, most people wouldn't think of it as something a thirty-seven-year-old would do. Yet I absolutely feel calmer and more centered after twenty minutes of drawing with my kids.

The point is that you never know what's going to work for what age, and your child's style and preferences are much more important than how old she is. That being said, you do want to think about your child's developmental stage when planning activities or interventions. Asking a five-year-old to sit quietly and notice her breath for ten minutes might be a stretch; young children usually do better with concrete, structured activities. Practicing a listening meditation with a ten-year-old might involve sitting together and just listening for five or ten minutes, while the same activity with a five-year-old might mean setting a timer for one or two minutes and asking her to listen for two sounds that she can report back to you at the end. If your child seems to be quickly losing interest in an activity, it may be because it's a little too old or too young for her.

It also can be tempting to reach for specific mindfulness tools when our kids are having a hard time. Sometimes that works, but not always. Children just can't learn new skills when they feel scared or hurt or angry, but they might be able to use skills they've been practicing all along. Just as you wouldn't throw a kid with no experience into the championship game and expect her to score the game-winning goal, you can't expect a screaming child to start breathing intentionally or listen to a guided meditation if she's never tried it before. While many of the practices and activities in this book will help your child get focused or calm down when she needs to, there are also many exercises that she can do when she is already in a good space. This is a crucial point: if you want your child to get present, centered, and grounded when she's stressed or angry or sad, you have to practice these skills with her when she's in a happy, open, and receptive mood.

Going Forward

Don't expect to do all of this on your own. Most adults who make mindfulness a core part of their lives have a supportive community to help them do it. Although the ideas behind mindfulness practice are simple, they're not always easy to implement. We humans, by nature, are forgetful and prone to daydreaming and worrying, and we love to multitask. We are distracted by technology and concerns about the future and regrets about the past, all of which make it difficult to stay in the present moment. As a result, we all need help doing this for ourselves and for our children. You may want to get involved in a meditation or mindfulness community for yourself, and yoga and mindfulness classes for children are becoming increasingly popular. I signed my girls (ages five and a half and four) up for a six-week class in which the teacher used music, dancing, picture books, and guided meditations to help the kids increase their bodily awareness and get in touch with their breathing.

Try not to feel too discouraged or frustrated at your child or yourself when you notice that you're falling into old habits, reacting thoughtlessly, or spacing out. As mindfulness teacher Sharon Salzberg (2010) reminds us, we can always, always begin again. The instant we notice that we've been a million miles away in our own minds is the moment when we have an opportunity to come back to the present moment and make a different choice, even if that happens a hundred times a day.

Finally, and most importantly, have fun with this. As the preeminent American mindfulness teacher Jon Kabat-Zinn has said, this mindfulness business is far too serious to be taken too seriously (Tippett 2009). Don't worry too much about doing it right, and don't let mindfulness be another task on your to-do list. Rather, try to find ways to organically integrate mindfulness into activities you already enjoy with your child. These practices can be a great way to enjoy parenting and reconnect with your child, as together you learn important skills that will help decrease your stress and increase your happiness.

PART 1

Getting Into A Mindful Mind-Set

CHAPTER 1

How Mindfulness Can Help Your Child

A few years ago, the *New York Times* ran an article about some fifth graders in Oakland, California, who were being taught mindfulness at school. The piece quoted a student named Tyran Williams, who defined mindfulness as "not hitting someone in the mouth" (Brown 2007). Tyran's words have been shared many times by teachers and writers in the mindfulness community, for several reasons. They're simple, straightforward, and practical, and they reflect what most parents want for our children: the ability to stop and pay attention to whatever we are doing long enough to realize that we are experiencing a big emotion and to then make a thoughtful and intentional choice about how we want to move forward. In this case, Tyran's mindfulness practice helped him to choose not to hit someone else.

This chapter will explore what mindfulness is, how it can help your child make good choices, and why it is so effective. I've included a number of exercises that you should feel free to try right away. First, though, let's talk about exactly what mindfulness is and isn't. There are a lot of misconceptions out there about mindfulness: that it's something mystical or spiritual, new agey or otherworldly, or that it requires us to spend hours in meditation so that we can develop the ability to clear our minds of all thoughts. While some folks may engage in mindfulness from these perspectives, I promise that you don't have to hang crystals or burn incense in the playroom (unless you want to), and you definitely don't need to clear your mind.

Perhaps the biggest misconception is that mindfulness is all about being happy or calm. While happiness and stress reduction are common and quite pleasant side effects of learning to be in the present moment without wishing it away, they are not the same thing as mindfulness. Fundamentally, mindfulness is about becoming aware of and accepting whatever is happening, which at times may involve sitting with painful or difficult emotions until they pass, as they will. It is a highly pragmatic practice that teaches us to see others and ourselves clearly so that we can make the most skillful choice possible in any given situation.

Try This: Find Your Breath

Mindfulness is fundamentally about getting out of our own minds and coming back into the present moment, into what is actually happening right here and right now. The simplest and most easily accessible way to do this is by focusing our attention on our breath. When we do this, we will let go of our anxieties, fears, fantasies, or wishes, if only for a moment. It's just not possible to pay attention to both things at once, and when we can get a little distance from our thoughts and feelings, we can also get a little clarity on what is actually happening right here and right now. So, for just one moment, I want you to notice where you feel your breath. It could be at the edge of your nose, in your nostrils, in the rising and falling of your chest, or in the movement of your belly. You don't have to do anything special; just notice it for a breath or two. This is an important first step in many different mindfulness practices.

A Formal Definition of Mindfulness

So what is mindfulness? There are many formal definitions out there—some spiritual, some secular, some quite scientific—but they all share a few common themes: *intention*, *attention*, *acceptance*, and *kindness*. Even though these are pretty big words for many children, the concepts behind them are relatively simple: choosing, noticing, being okay with whatever is actually happening, and being friendly to ourselves and others. The reality is that most kids already practice these skills far more frequently than we adults do, even if they don't realize it, and there's no reason for us to cloud their experience with overly complicated ideas. We just need to find the right language to help them understand what they are already doing, so they can be more intentional about it and so they have some useful words with which to explore their experience.

Here is how I like to explain mindfulness: *Mindfulness is about noticing what is happening right here and now, in a friendly and curious way, and then choosing what to do next.* I've adapted this definition from physician, mindfulness practitioner, mother, and author Amy Saltzman (2014). While it may seem like a relatively straightforward explanation, there are a number of important concepts in it that are worth exploring further.

Noticing

Noticing is about paying attention, which is the core practice of mindfulness. When we notice something, we become aware of it, and when we become aware, we are able to think more clearly about whatever is happening. This awareness gives us the freedom and space to consciously choose what we want to do next. This is a pretty simple idea, but getting there is no small feat. Most of us move through our lives being pretty spaced out. My husband headed off to work recently without his wallet; I've been to the grocery store three times this week and forgot to buy raisins—the one thing my daughters have been requesting—every time. How often has your child forgotten his homework folder or lost his mouth guard? When was the last time he hit another kid in the mouth because he just wasn't thinking about what he was doing?

A few weeks ago, I was cooking breakfast with my girls. My older daughter was standing on a stool in front of the stove, learning how to flip pancakes. Just then, her little sister wandered through the kitchen with a sparkly plastic comb. My big girl immediately jumped off the stool and went chasing after her sister, yelling that the comb was hers. She grabbed the comb and then immediately came back to the stove to help with the pancakes. She was so eager to resume cooking that she dropped the comb, without even thinking about where she was putting it, and it landed right in the flame. My daughter had been really focused when she was flipping the pancakes; it was a novel and challenging experience that easily kept her attention. But her sister and the sparkly comb easily distracted her. From that moment on, she was reacting to everything that happened without actually being aware of what she was doing; she was behaving mindlessly. She didn't even notice that she had dropped the toy that she had so desperately wanted just a few seconds earlier right into a fire. Fortunately, I was paying attention in that moment, and I turned off the stove and got the comb out before it started to melt or anything worse happened. In that moment, my daughter's attention was like most of our thoughts, easily pulled away at any time by whatever happens to distract us—a sparkly comb, a random memory, anything other than the present moment, no matter how important the present moment is.

When we pay attention by taking the time to notice what we are doing, we are less likely to make mistakes, drop and forget things, misinterpret situations, make incorrect assumptions, or overreact to situations that may not be as bad as they seem. In addition, we start to see others and ourselves clearly, we make more accurate assessments of situations and therefore better choices, and we give ourselves the opportunity to respond skillfully to new or challenging circumstances. Mindfulness helps us gain better control of our actions, which just isn't possible unless we notice what's happening in the first place.

Many children may have negative associations with ideas such as paying attention or focusing. This may be something that they have been told to do over and over again by their parents or teachers without really understanding what it means. But children know how to notice. They notice butterflies flitting around spring flowers, they notice backhoes and diggers from a mile away, they notice who gets picked last for teams, and they notice friends who make them feel included or excluded. They notice the angry looks that come across their parents' faces before we parents are even aware of what we're feeling. They notice worried thoughts and stomachaches. Children know how to notice, but just like all of us, they often forget to do so, especially when they're distracted, overwhelmed, confused, hungry, tired, or overcome by big or scary emotions, which is why teaching our children to pay attention—to choose to notice—is a core aspect of almost all of the practices in this book.

Try This: Noticing Walk

More than one parent I spoke with mentioned taking their children on walks outside for the sole purpose of noticing things. This is different from the walks to school or to the library or wherever; in this case, the point isn't to get somewhere or even anywhere. The point is just to notice, so if it takes you twenty minutes to walk half a block, that's great. Although any activity represents an opportunity to practice noticing, walking outside is particularly well suited because moving the body can help focus the mind, and you're not distracted by technology, clutter, toys to fight over, or laundry to fold. Older children might enjoy walking in silence or practicing a listening or observing meditation (see chapter 6). Younger children might need a little more structure; you can make a plan to notice three interesting things during the walk and then report back to each other at the end.

Here and Now

Most nights when I kiss my daughter goodnight, she has something important to tell me. Not important in the grand scheme of the universe, but important to her in that moment. Important enough that if she doesn't tell me, she'll have a hard time falling asleep. Sometimes it's a sad thought about a time when I got upset with her earlier in the day, a worry about whether or not she'll get a chance to finish a project at school tomorrow, or a memory of something that happened six months ago. Rarely is it an observation about what is happening for her in that particular moment. That's just not where her brain tends to go.

It's not only my little girl, of course, but me as well and almost everyone I know. If you were to ask most folks what they were thinking at any given moment, chances are they'd be worrying about something that may or may not happen in the future, stressing about or regretting something that has already happened, or feeling frustrated or annoyed with a person or situation they can't change but are desperately trying to control anyway. Having these less than helpful thoughts doesn't mean there's anything wrong with any of us. It just means we're human.

There are many reasons why our minds tend to focus on the past or the future—anywhere but right here and now. Once upon a time, the ability to remember that a saber-toothed tiger ate Cousin Joe and to make a plan to avoid that tiger in the future was a crucial part of staying alive. Those cavemen and women who were unable to keep a mental list of potential threats and do what was necessary to avoid them weren't going to last very long. The same holds true in certain situations today: the memory of a child's first allergic reaction to peanuts motivates his parents to plan ahead and bring a nut-free cupcake to the next birthday party. A child's ability to remember how hot the stove was when he touched it the first time keeps him from getting burned again. The problem is that our brains don't know when to stop with all the planning and remembering, and we end up spending far too much of our mental space analyzing the past and trying to predict the future in ways that aren't particularly helpful. In addition to the obvious problem that we can't change what's already happened or what's coming next, each time our minds wander, it means we aren't paying attention to the present moment; we're likely reacting to whatever is going on in our wandering minds instead of responding to what is actually happening right in front of us. And that's where we get into trouble.

Here's a typical example from my house. My daughters got into it yesterday over a Barbie crown. I'm talking about a screaming, swiping, code red, pissed-off fight. First, I separated the girls to make sure they couldn't hurt each other, and then I gave them each their favorite soft toy to snuggle—a physical cue to help them calm down. We sat quietly for a minute or two, and once they were calm enough to talk, they began to tell me what was going on.

"She stole my crown! She always steals my stuff! She stole my Dora doll last night, too!"

"It's not hers! It's mine! I need my sparkly Barbie crown, so Barbie can go to the ball!"

As I listened to their words, I looked at the array of Barbie paraphernalia on our living room rug. In the middle of it all, I saw two crowns. Both sparkly, both pink.

The girls had forgotten all about the second crown. They had gotten so caught up in all the past injustices they had experienced, the importance of their plan for the game going forward, and their need to have everything they wanted that they couldn't see what was right in front of them.

This is a pretty common scene in my house and many other homes; and unfortunately, a second sparkly Barbie crown isn't going to appear each time our children feel like they're being treated unfairly. In fact, our best shot at responding skillfully to challenging situations is to do whatever we can to let go of the past and the future and stay as focused as we can on what is actually happening, right here and right now.

Try This: Stop, Drop, and Breathe

This is an easy, quick, and funny way to disrupt a difficult or unhelpful situation and to breathe your way back into the present moment. Whenever you find yourself or your child spinning out of control, lost in thoughts, or overwhelmed by emotions, remember to stop, drop, and breathe: stop, drop whatever you are doing, and breathe deeply and intentionally. I've even been known to literally drop to the floor—a move that never fails to disrupt a difficult moment and get my children laughing, regardless of how grumpy we all feel.

Being Friendly and Curious

The third part of the mindfulness definition is about adopting a friendly and curious attitude in response to whatever comes our way. Let me give you an example.

My girls and I were out running errands the other day when we saw a little boy with a large, dark birthmark on his face. Almost immediately I began worrying about him. "Oh, that poor thing," I thought to myself "He's going to have such a hard time in life. I hope the other children aren't mean to him. They were so awful to me when I had acne in middle school." Meanwhile, my daughters were staring at him. I tried to distract them, as I didn't want the boy to feel bad. A moment later, my older daughter was pulling at my sleeve. "Mommy, that boy is so interesting to me. He looks a little different. What does he have on his face? I really like how it looks."

My daughter's words stopped me in my tracks and jerked me out of my own mind. I had been concerned about my girls staring because I had assumed they were judging the boy, and I was worried they might say something mean or disrespectful. It's never nice to be stared at, to be sure, and I'm still teaching them not to stare. In this case, however, my daughter was being curious. Her words weren't hurtful at all. In fact, at the end, they were quite nice. She had just seen something new, and she wanted to understand more about it. Some folks in the mindfulness world refer to this as *beginner's mind*, when we are able to approach a situation without all the judgments and preconceptions and assumptions and worries that most people have about almost everything. I, on the other hand, had just the opposite of beginner's mind. I assumed this little boy would have a horrible time in life because of his birthmark. We never did talk to him, but I can guarantee you that my daughter's open mind would have made for a much kinder, more interesting, and more enlightening conversation than my worried and presumptive thoughts.

The reality is that most of the time when something happens, we judge it. We decide that it's great or it's terrible, or it's somewhere in between: perhaps okay or good enough, a little annoying, or fairly uninteresting. On the face of it, these judgments aren't such a bad thing, and sometimes they're actually quite helpful, such as when we judge a situation to be unsafe for our children and ourselves and we make the choice to leave. More often than not, however, each time we pass judgment about whatever is going on, we are immediately inserting a layer of thoughts, fears, concerns, and comparisons between ourselves and what's really happening. We are closing ourselves off to learning more about our experience, and we're sending a message to others and ourselves that whatever is happening really isn't okay.

Just the other day, my friend's son—an incredibly smart and capable fourth grader—announced that he is terrible at math. Regardless of whether or not math is his best subject, each time he tells himself or someone else that he's no good at it, he is strengthening his belief that he isn't good at it, which will certainly impact his ability to be successful in math class. What if he could notice those thoughts, let go of them, and decide not to worry about whether or not he's good at math but to just get curious about the math problem in front of him at that moment? Now he may or may not end up majoring in math in college, but either way, his experience of math class, and of himself, is going to be much more accurate and likely more pleasant.

The concept of friendly curiosity or kindness is central to mindfulness, as we all too often ask questions about situations in a fairly negative or judgmental way. It's the difference between asking "What's wrong with you?" and asking "What's going on right now? How can I understand this better? How can I help?" It doesn't matter how much attention we are paying or how interested we may be, if our perspective is clouded by annoyance, anger, or frustration. Mindfulness is fundamentally about kind attention, and the truth is that there are few situations in life that we can't respond to in a friendly and curious way. Whatever is going on, we can welcome and accept it and try to understand it more. When we are able to do that, we can see the situation and our role in it more clearly, and we can make better choices.

Try This: Be the Scientist

Scientists are all about asking questions, with the sole purpose of getting a clear and accurate understanding of a situation or phenomenon, rather than trying to force a certain outcome. One way to help our children get curious is to encourage them to take a scientific approach to whatever is bothering them. We were recently on vacation with another family, and their six-year-old boy was having a hard time falling asleep in a new house because of the creaking in the walls. This boy is particularly interested in science, so I encouraged him to be a scientist and count the creaks to see how many he could hear. Counting the creaks shifted his attention from anxiety to interest, and he soon relaxed and fell asleep. The next time you or your child are annoyed by something you see, hear, or smell, try getting curious about it instead. You'll soon find that you can't be curious and angry (or whatever the big feeling is) at the same time. The big emotions will pass more quickly, and you might even get some useful information about how to proceed.

Choosing What to Do Next

This is the pot of gold at the end of the mindfulness rainbow—what every parent who picked up this book is looking for—how to teach our children to make thoughtful, intentional choices about their behavior instead of freaking out like a little Tasmanian devil with his head on fire every time we serve peas for dinner. As we all know, making good choices can be an incredibly challenging thing for our kids to do, especially when they're tired, hungry, stressed, or overwhelmed. Fortunately for all of us, it is possible to help our children get to this place—and not just through scare tactics or sheer force of will, both of which may seem effective in the moment but will surely backfire in the long run.

Many of the challenging situations our children face happen when things aren't going their way. They can't have the toy they desire, they got a new baby brother or sister whom they don't want, they have to do homework or clean the kitchen when they'd rather play video games, or their parents are getting divorced. The list goes on and on. The natural human reaction to an unpleasant situation is to fight it, perhaps by grabbing that toy out of a friend's hand, trying to convince Mom and Dad to return the baby to the hospital, procrastinating on homework, or raging at their parents. These knee-jerk reactions can lead to bigger problems—time-outs, being grounded, explosive fights with siblings, angry parents, tense relationships, sleep problems, and academic challenges, to name a few—and rarely do they solve anything. However, that doesn't usually stop our children from reacting that way, because it is human nature to try to make unpleasant feelings go away.

When we can help our children take a mindful approach to life by noticing what is happening in a friendly and curious way, over and over again, they learn how to accept difficult situations. This acceptance is not only significantly less painful than fighting against reality but also a lot more effective. To be clear, I'm not talking about a passive, powerless acceptance. I'm talking about acknowledging what is actually happening, so we can free up all that head space we were spending denying, rejecting, refusing, or trying to change reality. When we do that, we have a lot more mental and emotional energy to devote to what to do next. We get out of the past and into the present, which is the only place where we actually can effect change.

The struggle over homework is a good example. Most kids don't want to do homework. They've been sitting in chairs all day, trying to pay attention to something they may or may not find particularly interesting, and then they get home and are expected to do the same thing all over again. Maybe they're tired or hungry, bored by the work, stressed by the length or difficulty of the assignment, or confused about where to start. We parents are also often tired and stressed after a long day at work or with the kids, and we might be worried about our child's academic performance, bored and frustrated by the constant homework negotiations and battles, or feeling pulled in ten different directions as we try to make dinner, wrangle the other children, and keep our kid focused on his spelling words. You probably know how this scene often plays out: parent nags, kid procrastinates, parent nags more, maybe yells or threatens, kid gets either angry or sad, and the whole thing blows up. The homework doesn't get done, and the level of tension and frustration in the house shoots way up, which only reinforces everyone's dislike of homework, thus guaranteeing another miserable day tomorrow.

Here's how it can look different when both parents and children take a mindful approach to the homework debacle. Say you ask your child to do his homework. Maybe he sits down at the table; maybe he doesn't. Either way, at some step in the process, you realize that your son isn't interested in his spelling words. You notice yourself starting to nag, and you stop. You take a deep breath and a moment to assess the situation, and you realize you don't actually know what's going on for your son, other than his lack of desire to finish his worksheet. Again, you can either fight this (perhaps with nags or threats), or you can accept it. Once you accept it, you can get curious about it. "So, I see you don't want to do your spelling. What's going on? What do you need to be able to do this right now?" By asking these questions, you are teaching your son to get curious about his own experience rather than just react before he knows what's actually going on.

You may get a number of different answers: maybe he had a bad day at school, maybe he's hungry or tired, maybe he's confused by the assignment, or maybe he just plain hates spelling. When you ask those questions, you are helping your son get some clarity about what he is dealing with in the moment. From there, you can decide together how to proceed; perhaps he simply needs a snack or a night off from spelling, maybe he needs a different approach to homework, or maybe he needs a little tutoring. The point is that you didn't lose your cool or get in a fight with your child; you modeled a mindful response for him, and hopefully you actually solved the problem. The trick here was noticing what was going on, accepting that this is what's actually happening now, and getting curious about it. That mental stance created enough space for both of you to make a different and better choice about what to do next.

(It's important to note that conversations and logic might work well with older children but not so well with little ones. In those situations, it's your job to stay as calm as you can and do your best to figure out what your child needs. This isn't easy to do, and you aren't always going to get it right. That's okay. This is an ongoing practice that you can keep coming back to, and both you and your child will get better at it.)

One thing you might notice about the homework example is that it started with you, the parent, getting to a mindful place. This is a crucial point that will be explored more in the next chapter: we can't help our children practice mindfulness unless we are doing it ourselves or at least with them. Reminding your kid to take deep breaths isn't going to be terribly effective if you bark it at him as you're taking dinner out of the oven and trying to finish up a phone call from work. In that case, you're still fighting with reality, even if you're using the words, but not the intention, of mindfulness to do it.

Try This: STOP

Sometimes when we're in a rut, it can be hard to know how to come back to the present moment and then how to move forward. My favorite practice when I feel lost or unsure is to just STOP, which stands for Stop, Take a Breath, Observe, and Proceed. See how this works for you: Stop whatever you're doing, Take a deep breath, spend a few moments Observing what is going within you and around you, and then Proceed from that place of calm awareness. Try this a few times and see how it works for you before you introduce it to your child. If it seems to be working, you may want to color a few STOP signs with your child and hang them around the house.

The Benefits of Mindfulness

Hopefully by now you have a reasonably clear sense of the core aspects of mindfulness—noticing the here and now in a friendly and curious way so you can choose what to do next—and a good sense of how it works. The best way to truly understand mindfulness is to practice it and then notice how you and your child think, feel, and respond differently to challenging situations. You may also have realized by now that mindfulness isn't a quick fix; it's neither a star chart that will entice your child with the promise of a new toy into behaving nor a threat that will scare him into complacency. It's an ongoing practice of planting seeds that will eventually sprout and grow and serve your child incredibly well. The good news is that you don't have to wait long. The parents I interviewed reported a range of benefits for their children that they attributed to ongoing mindfulness practices with them. Here are a few:

- Growing awareness of their bodies, thoughts, and emotions and an increased vocabulary with which to talk about what they are experiencing, thinking, and feeling
- Increased resilience, including the ability to soothe themselves, calm down faster, and regulate their own emotions
- Stronger sense of other people's thoughts and emotions, and increased empathy for others
- Improved concentration and ability to focus
- Better sleep
- Increased confidence in themselves, their ideas, and their preferences
- Decreased anxiety and depression
- Increased ability to be fully present with themselves and with others (which leads to better social skills and stronger relationships)

Overall, these parents reported that they felt more connected to their children and that their children were generally calmer and happier as a result of learning to pause for a moment, catch their breath, and get a sense of what they really need.

Try This: Plant a Garden

Plant a garden together or even a flower. The metaphor of planting seeds and waiting patiently for them to grow is a useful way to think about the work you are doing when you teach mindfulness to your child. You can't expect an immediate response (although sometimes that does happen), and you need to trust that over time the ideas you are sharing will take root and grow. Taking the time to actually plant some seeds with your kid is a wonderful way to demonstrate many of the concepts associated with mindfulness:

- **Kindness.** This is a central theme in mindfulness practice and inherent in caring for another living thing, including flowers and plants.
- **Curiosity.** Questions such as what the plants need, whether or not they will grow, and how to best care for them will help reinforce the attitude of curiosity that is so important to mindfulness.
- **Knowledge that everything changes.** Observing the life cycle of plants reinforces this basic idea. The reality of life is that everything changes and nothing lasts forever. Remembering that this, too, shall pass is a useful way to manage difficult situations and emotions and fully appreciate beautiful moments.

Planting a garden offers us an opportunity to slow down and use many of our senses, including feeling the soil, observing the growth of plants, smelling flowers, and tasting the vegetables. The slow pace of tending to plants can be a powerful antidote to the speed of daily life, and spending time outdoors can help us get a break from the clutter that can so often take up way too much space in our homes and our brains.

The parents I interviewed are not the only ones who've seen the benefits for their children; hundreds of studies have investigated the impact of mindfulness training on diverse groups of children, from preschoolers to adolescents. Just to give you a few examples, researchers found that children who were taught basic mindfulness skills (including mindful breathing, basic meditations, and yoga) had significant improvements in these areas:

- Self-control and overall ability to regulate behavior (Razza, Bergen-Cico, and Raymond 2015)
- Problem-solving (Flook et al. 2010)
- Awareness of their own thought processes (Flook et al. 2010)
- Attention (Black and Fernando 2014)
- Respect for others (Black and Fernando 2014)
- Self-esteem (Tan and Martin 2015)
- Sleep (Bei et al. 2013)

Finally, children who learned mindfulness reported decreased symptoms of depression and anxiety as well as fewer repetitive, anxious thoughts (Ames et al. 2014; Kuyken et al. 2013; Mendelson et al. 2010).

You may be wondering how a practice as simple as mindfulness could lead to such a wide range of benefits for your child.

Can learning how to focus our attention in a kind and curious way really lead to such significant changes? It can, and here's how.

How Mindfulness Actually Works

There are several ways to understand how and why mindfulness works, and most of them have to do with the difference between noticing and choosing our experience and getting lost in it. Here are a few ways to understand what's going on.

Learning to Pay Attention to Just One Thing

On the most basic level, mindfulness practice calls on us to focus our attention on whatever we are doing and to notice when our minds have wandered so we can bring them back again. This is a radical departure from modern society's glorification of multitasking, a habit that our children seem to adopt at a rapid pace, especially when it comes to technology. For some kids, it's the flashing screen that's always on in the background. For other kids, it's another distraction, such as eating or talking through any activity. Whether it's watching TV, snacking on pretzels, or telling an endless story about the latest playground drama, what it means is that they aren't paying full attention to whatever else they may be doing. Multitasking comes quite easily to most children, whether they mean to do it or not, because it distracts them from the boredom or the difficulty of whatever else they are doing and because it's what the human mind wants to do anyway. But the truth is that our brains aren't good at jumping from one thing to the next. As neuroscientists have found, we can't actually do more than one thing at once; instead we switch rapidly from one stimulus to another—from screen to book to food and back again—which means that no one thing gets our full attention (Salvucci and Taatgen 2010). The end result is that we don't do any one thing well, we're more likely to make mistakes, and we end up feeling increasingly stressed from our brains jumping around all day, never resting on just one thing. The focused attention of mindfulness is a powerful antidote to this phenomenon and can help decrease the stress levels that often build up after extended periods of multitasking.

You Are Not Your Thoughts

When children practice watching their thoughts and then letting them go so that they can return to the present moment, they learn that they are not their thoughts and that they have the power to choose which thoughts to keep and which ones to let go of. The fact is that our brains have a tendency to think constantly, no matter what else we are doing. We're never going to stop this process, and stopping it is not what mindfulness is all about. The problem isn't with the thinking; the problem is that most of us have a tendency to take seriously every thought that happens to cross our minds, regardless of its quality, accuracy, relevance, or helpfulness. We get easily wrapped up in the ideas that cross our minds, and we can, and do, devote an inordinate amount of time and energy to exploring, understanding, deconstructing, conquering, or defeating them. Rarely does this process give us clarity; more often than not, it sucks us deeper into the rabbit holes that are our brains and further away from our actual experience, which is the only place where we can really effect change in our lives. The truth is that thoughts are just thoughts—they aren't reality, and they dictate our reality only if we allow them to.

Some Buddhist traditions refer to our scattered, confused, inconsistent, and restless minds as *monkey mind*. A mindful approach can help our children get a little distance from their monkey minds (the parts of their brains that are reactive, unpredictable, and generally unhelpful), so they can get some perspective on what is really going on and what their choices are for moving forward.

Try This: Don't Let the Monkey Drive the Bus

I got this idea from the popular children's book *Don't Let the Pigeon Drive the Bus* by Mo Willems (2003). Sometimes our brains are so busy screeching at us and flinging thoughts all over the place that it's like we have a monkey running around in our minds and driving our thoughts. Just as we wouldn't let a pigeon drive a bus, we shouldn't let a monkey determine how we pay attention and what we pay attention to. You can introduce this idea to your child through the use of picture books (see the resources list for examples), and whenever you notice that your child's thoughts seem totally out of control, you may want to ask if the monkey is driving the bus. If so, maybe it's time to have him ride in the back for a while. This is a funny way to remind your child to calm down without shaming or dismissing his experience.

Identifying Feelings

Whereas our thoughts live in our minds, our feelings tend to take root in our bodies. Not unlike most adults, children can get so wrapped up in their thinking that they often don't notice the tension in their shoulders or the queasiness in their tummies, and if they do notice, they may not be sure what it means or how it is impacting their behavior. Many of the practices in this book are designed to teach our children to pay attention to what is happening in their bodies and to begin to connect those sensations to the emotions and thoughts they may be having. Once they can learn what their bodies are telling them, children can get a better sense of how they are feeling and what they need before things really fall apart for them.

There are many ways to help our kids learn to identify their feelings, and later chapters will cover this in more detail. You can start, though, by intentionally using words to describe the emotions you think your child is having, by reading and discussing books about feelings (several are listed in the resources section), or by asking your child to draw what he is feeling. Finally, you can help your child get more in touch with the sensations in his body, either by asking him directly or by asking him how a favorite stuffed animal or toy robot's body is feeling.

Try This: Get CALM

The body scan is a traditional mindfulness meditation practice in which you scan your attention over your entire body, noticing how each part of your body feels. You may choose to try to relax tense spots, but you don't have to. Fundamentally, this practice is about noticing. Going through your entire body can be a tall order for a kid, so you can focus on helping your child get CALM, which stands for Chest, Arms, Legs, and Mind.

Have your child sit, stand, or lie down in a comfortable position and ask him to notice what his chest feels like. Let him know that he can tell you or he can just notice it in his mind. If he can't put words to the sensation, that's okay too. He can just notice it. Then ask him to notice his arms and legs, and finally, can he pay attention to what's happening in his mind? What is he thinking? What ideas or questions are moving through his mind? You don't need to give him any feedback or suggestions about his sensations or thoughts; whatever they are, they are okay. Simply listen and be with him as you help him notice the different parts of his body.

This Too Shall Pass

Regardless of what our experience is and whether it lives in our bodies or in our minds, the reality is that it won't last forever. However, the opposite can often feel true, especially to our children whenever they're dealing with a tough situation, whether it's a terrible cold, a difficult social interaction, or an interminable math class. They can get stuck in repetitive or obsessive thoughts about whatever is happening, or they can get so caught up in their mental drama that they lose touch with what is really going on. When we help our children take a mindful approach to situations, they are more likely to notice that thoughts, feelings, and physical sensations arise and then pass, which can help make difficult situations more tolerable. It can also help our children learn to enjoy and take full advantage of the positive moments in life, which they often miss because they're too distracted, anxious, or getting all agitated about some tiny detail that isn't right. Finally, when our kids learn over and over again that nothing is permanent, they will get more skillful at managing transitions or unexpected changes.

Mindfulness Helps Train the Brain

Perhaps most importantly for our children, mindfulness helps train the brain to respond more effectively to stressful situations, which is especially important for developing minds. We know now that our brains continue to develop and change throughout our lives, and much of that change is determined by what we do. Our brains are made up of billions of neurons, which send electrical signals to each other through trillions of different connections with other neurons. I like to think of each neuron as a piece of train track and of the electrical signals as trains. Neuroscientists like to say that neurons that fire together wire together, which means that the more often we utilize and make connections between different parts of our brains, the stronger and faster those connections will become. We see this process at work when our children learn to play a sport, for example. At first they may struggle to make contact with the soccer ball, and they can't quite figure out how to kick it, but with practice, their minds and bodies learn to work together until they no longer need to think about how to kick the ball; they just do it. The same happens with mindfulness.

Each time our children practice mindfulness, perhaps by focusing on the sounds around them for a few minutes or by stopping to take a deep breath before they act rashly, they are actually changing their brains. Recent research (Hölzel et al. 2011) has found that mindfulness meditation can reduce the size of our limbic system (the fight, flee, freeze, or freak-out part of the brain responsible for scanning the environment for threats, real or imagined, and then reacting to them) while the prefrontal cortex (the part of the brain that helps us calm down, think clearly, plan ahead, and make rational decisions) gets stronger and bigger. This sort of brain change can be especially useful for children, as their prefrontal cortexes won't be fully developed until their early twenties. In fact, this part of the brain barely exists in young toddlers, which is why you can't argue logic with them—they don't quite understand it—and why they can lose it at every little thing. Now, it's unlikely that most of our children will be meditating for half an hour every day, but make no mistake about it: the more they practice the skills of intention, attention, kindness, and acceptance, the more quickly and easily those skills will come to them in difficult moments, because of the changes they are making in their brains.

Try This: Explain the Brain

Children are often more responsive to suggestions if they understand why we are making them in the first place. Teaching children about how their brains function and change is a great place to start. I love the description in *Little Flower Yoga for Kids*, in which author Jennifer Cohen Harper (2013, 8–10) talks about the difference between "the protective brain" (the limbic system) and "the thoughtful brain" (the prefrontal cortex). The protective brain works hard to keep us as safe and happy as possible, but sometimes it doesn't think things through. That's why we need the thoughtful brain to help us slow down and make the best choices. Mindfulness helps the protective brain calm down, so the thoughtful brain can have a turn.

Hopefully by now you have a better sense of how mindfulness helped young Tyran make the decision to not hit someone in the mouth. Although he doesn't go into detail, my guess is that by paying attention to his experience as it was in that moment, rather than getting hijacked by his frustrated or angry thoughts and then reacting to them, Tyran was able to notice that he was getting mad, before he exploded. By responding to that awareness with some degree of interest or curiosity, rather than dismissing it and charging ahead angrily, he gave himself just enough head space to make a different choice, a more skillful choice. That moment, when something has happened and we notice that it has happened, whatever it may be, is the moment when everything can change. Teaching mindfulness to our children is all about helping them learn to pay more attention to what is actually happening within and around them, so they can notice what is happening, before they get too wrapped up in their mental spinning, and make a better choice. The first and most important step in teaching our kids how to do this involves learning how to do it ourselves, which is the subject of the next chapter.

CHAPTER 2

It All Starts with You

This chapter will talk about why practicing mindfulness yourself is the single most important step you can take in teaching it to your child. Don't stress if you've never taken an intentional breath in your life or if you've never meditated; I'll walk you through everything you need to know to get started. But first, I'd like to tell you how I got started with mindfulness and what I've learned from it.

When people find out that I practice and teach mindfulness and mindful parenting, they often ask how I got into meditation and mindfulness. They're probably expecting me to share a story of some spiritual quest for deeper meaning in life, as they often look surprised when I tell them that I was just trying to figure out how to yell at my kids less often. Before my younger daughter was even two years old, I found that I was losing my temper with the girls more often than I felt comfortable with. I started doing research on how to stop yelling, and everything I read suggested starting a mindfulness meditation practice. I had no interest in meditating. In my mind, meditation was for space cadets with no direction in life. The thing is, nothing else was working. Eventually, I got over myself and took a course in mindfulness-based stress reduction, and I learned the basics of mindfulness, meditation, and yoga. Much to my shock, I wasn't yelling as much. I soon realized that my practice was impacting my children as well—the calmer I was, the calmer they were.

As I've already mentioned, one of the best ways we can teach our children is by practicing what we want them to learn. Perhaps you already have a mindfulness practice, which may involve regular meditation, yoga, or mindful check-ins throughout the day, and that's what drew you to this book. If that's the case, then you probably understand that mindfulness is much more than just a set of tools or tips. It's a way of approaching the world with awareness, acceptance, and kindness, which can help you stay steady and focused when everything around you seems to be going crazy. You also may have noticed that this practice helps you remain calmer and less reactive when your child is pushing your buttons and that your parenting is much more effective and empathic when you don't get swept up in every one of your child's tantrums or rage storms. If you only recently started a mindfulness practice, you may be noticing ways in which your kid seems to be responding to these changes in you; perhaps she's freaking out less often or less intensely or she's recovering more quickly, even if you haven't been teaching her mindfulness skills directly.

Or maybe none of this is the case. Perhaps you didn't know much about mindfulness before you picked up this book, or you had a few preconceived notions that may or may not be accurate. Maybe you think mindfulness could be helpful for you, but you're not sure where to start. Or maybe you think it might be a good idea for your child, but it just doesn't seem like the right match for you. Maybe you've tried meditating before, and you felt like it didn't work, or perhaps the exercises seemed too contrived or challenging. I understand those thoughts and feelings, as I've had them all myself. Whatever the case, something about mindfulness has piqued your interest, because you're reading this book. I would encourage you to keep an open mind about the role mindfulness can play in your life, because the reality is that we can't teach this stuff to our children effectively unless we are doing it ourselves.

Now before you freak out about this, take a deep breath or two. (No, really. Take a few deep breaths. It's a basic mindfulness practice, and essentially what you'll be doing by the end of this chapter.) You don't have to move to an ashram on the top of a mountain, head off on a ten-day silent retreat, or spend several hours each day sitting cross-legged on the floor chanting, but you do need to give this mindfulness thing a shot if you're hoping to share it with your child. I'll talk more about what that will look like, but first let's explore why having your own practice is fundamental to teaching it to others.

Try This: Three Magic Breaths

Several different basic breathing practices are included in this book, as breathing is a fundamental first step to getting into a place of mindful awareness. This exercise introduces one of them.

At any point during the day, if you or your child is feeling frazzled, frustrated, or overwhelmed, you can take three magic breaths together. This just means stopping whatever you are doing and taking three deep, intentional breaths. I suggest you breathe in and out through your nose, but you can do it any way that feels comfortable and calming to you. Notice how you feel afterward—hopefully you feel a bit calmer, more grounded, and better able to move forward with your day.

Why We Can't Just Tell Our Kids to Relax

You have no idea how much I would love to be able to just tell my daughters to calm down or to hand them a snow globe to stare at each time they're stressed or sad or scared. More often than not, I'm already overwhelmed by just trying to keep my own cool as we all get through the day, and I don't have the energy or desire to deal with their rough patches. In my more tired moments, I want them to just go away, pull themselves together, and then come find me when they're back to their sweet, helpful little selves. Sadly, it rarely works that way for me or any parent I know. We can't just tell our kids to relax every time they're sad, frustrated, or angry; we need our own mindfulness practice if we hope to teach our kids. This is true for several reasons.

Our Kids Know When We're Not Being Real with Them

The first reason is pretty simple and straightforward: children can spot a phony from a mile away, especially if that phony happens to be their parent. They have finely tuned radar for every single one of our inconsistencies and hypocrisies, and they will call us out on them in any way they can. This is a major bummer for us parents for several reasons, but in this particular case, it means that if we are asking them to do something (mindful breathing, guided meditations, and so on) that they know we don't do ourselves, they're likely to either refuse or merely go through the motions because they have no other choice—just the opposite of what we were hoping to achieve. Alternately, our children know without a doubt when we are being honest with them, and they are much more likely to respect us and respond to us when we are trying to connect from a place of authenticity and compassion. In addition, our children are deeply curious about our lives and how we spend our time, and if they know that mindfulness is important to us, they'll probably want to know more about it, especially if we share it with them in thoughtful and respectful ways.

The "Eat Your Vegetables" Rule

This brings me to the second reason why we can't just tell our kids to be mindful. I think of it as the "eat your veggies" rule. My husband loves vegetables and eats them all the time, whereas I have worked hard over the years to learn to tolerate them enough to eat them on a regular basis. Occasionally, my husband will kindly and casually suggest that I should have a salad for lunch instead of a tuna sandwich. He's definitely practicing what he's preaching, and I know it. I also know that he's right, but I usually go ahead and eat my sandwich anyway. This dynamic has little to do with our individual personalities or the quality of our marriage. It's about human nature. People don't like to be told what to do, even when the suggestions are coming from those who love us, who want the best for us, and who are right. We want to feel like we're in control of our lives and our choices, and we'll even go so far as to make choices for ourselves that are bad, or less than great, if it gives us that much-desired sense of self-empowerment. Even the most benign, reasonable, and well-intentioned suggestions can be perceived as threats to our autonomy, and even the most mature and thoughtful among us can end up reacting from a need to feel powerful and independent rather than responding to the value of the idea being presented. (I think it's fair to say that most children wouldn't qualify for the description of "the most mature and thoughtful among us." Mine certainly wouldn't. Most of the time, I wouldn't either.)

Any parent who has ever made a suggestion to her child knows exactly what I'm talking about. Nowhere is the push and pull for autonomy more powerful than between kids and their parents; we're motivated by an endless sense of responsibility to help our children be as healthy, safe, and happy as possible, while they're engaged in an ongoing developmental quest to exert their own power. If mindfulness is a part of your life and your child knows it, chances are she will be interested when you suggest a new practice, game, or activity to try—especially if you're willing to do it with her. But it's also possible, depending on your mood, your child's developmental stage, or even the phases of the moon, that your suggestion to take three magic breaths will be about as effective as my husband's telling me to eat a salad, which is to say, not very. Although our goal is ultimately to strike a balance between teaching our children directly and making a point to model it for them, sometimes we need to back off on the explicit teaching part and stay focused on our own practice—whether we're talking about eating vegetables or meditation. When we stay consistent with what matters to us, in all likelihood, our kids will eventually get interested enough to try it on their own. It may not happen until they've grown up and moved out, but at least we've planted the seeds.

We Can't Teach What We Haven't Experienced

The last and most important reason we need to have our own mindfulness practice is that it's the only way to get a clear and accurate sense of what it's really about and how it actually works. Mindfulness is one of those things that you can't teach other people if you haven't tried it yourself. There are a ton of misconceptions about what it means to pay attention to the present moment with kindness and acceptance, and regardless of how many books we may read about it (including this one), mindfulness is not something we can understand by thinking about it.

It's like trying to teach your child to swim when you have never jumped into the pool yourself. You may have read every book on the shelf about how to hold your body so you can float, the motions of the different strokes, when to inhale, and how to exhale through your nose so you don't breathe in water, but until you've actually been underwater, felt the water all around you, and realized you couldn't breathe—but you stayed calm enough to get your head above water when you needed to, so you could breathe properly—you're not going to understand anything about what your kid is going through as she flails around in the pool and what she might need to feel safe and be successful.

When you suggest that your kid try a mindfulness practice when you haven't done it yourself, it's like handing your child a life preserver and pretending that's swimming. You're giving her a generic tool that may or may not be effective in the moment, but it's unlikely to be something she will eventually internalize. As a result, she'll likely do whatever she can to avoid her big feelings, and when that doesn't work, she'll feel like she's drowning and may end up flailing and choking. Fortunately, you can decide to get in the pool, practice for yourself, and notice how it feels. This is the best way to teach your kid, and you get the bonus of all the amazing benefits of mindfulness.

Try This: Connection Before Correction

"Connection before correction" is a common phrase in the parenting literature, but it applies to virtually all social interactions. Basically, it means that other people are more likely to accept your feedback and suggestions if they feel connected to you. This is precisely why you can't just tell your child to go breathe when she's having a tough moment, but if you can take the time to connect, if only for a second, and understand what's going on with her, she will be more likely to accept such a suggestion. So the next time your child is having a hard time, take a few deep breaths and calm yourself down so you can connect before you correct.

Starting Your Own Mindfulness Practice

The best way to learn to practice mindfulness is to start by doing it when you're relatively calm and unruffled so that when you're in the middle of a difficult moment—whether your own or your child's—you have at least some experience with mindfulness's benefits and challenges. This is also how you'll want to teach the practice to your child. If you share the ideas and exercises when she's in a good space, she'll be much more likely to get a handle on it than if you try when she's overwhelmed by anxiety, anger, or exhaustion.

There are two basic ways to practice mindfulness: formally and informally. Formal mindfulness practice is the same thing as *meditation*, which is just a fancy word for setting aside a period of time each day with the intention of doing nothing more than paying attention to just one thing. You may choose to focus on the sounds around you, your own breathing, the steps you take while walking, or your bodily sensations, for example. Informal mindfulness is the practice of bringing our full awareness to whatever we may be doing throughout the course of a day, whether it's showering, sitting in a work meeting, holding our son as he's getting a painful shot, watching our daughter's hockey game, or having a much-needed dinner out with our partner or friend.

Any time we practice meditation and mindfulness, our minds will wander frequently—as often as every few seconds, in fact. This is normal. Our minds were built to think, consider, plan, analyze, worry, anticipate, and, mostly, try to figure out how to get more of the good stuff and how to get away from anything unpleasant or even slightly boring. The goal of mindfulness is not to stop this process. That's never going to happen, not for any of us. Whether we're sitting on a meditation cushion or stirring the soup, the goal is just to notice, in a friendly, accepting way, that our mind has traveled a million miles away and to bring it back to the sounds around us, our breath, our steps, or our bodies.

By noticing our thoughts and getting some distance from them, over and over again, we learn that we are not our thoughts. When we realize that our thoughts are not our reality, we can choose whether or not we want to engage with them. Rather than getting caught up in and overwhelmed by our fantasies and worries, we can notice them just as we might notice cars driving by. We don't have to hitch a ride with every single car that happens to cross our path; we can choose which car is headed in the direction we actually want to go, and let the rest of them drive on by. When we come to truly understand that we have a choice in how we respond to ourselves and our children, we realize that we are free to make the most skillful choice possible and we can teach our children how to do the same. And each time we don't make that best choice, we can learn to forgive ourselves with humor and kindness. The first step, though, is to get a little distance from our own thoughts.

There are several specific practices you can try, both formal and informal. What follows are some common meditations to get you started; there are also many books, CDs, and websites available with a range of guided meditations (see resources). If you have other meditations that you prefer, maybe based in your religious or faith tradition, that's great too. Most importantly, remember that meditating can, and should, be a pleasant experience. As Karen Maezen Miller (2009), a mother, writer, and Zen Buddhist priest, says so eloquently, "The point of meditation is not pain. Your life is painful enough as it is. The point of meditation is to relieve pain." I encourage you to try out a few of these practices, even just for a few minutes at a time, and see what works for you.

Formal Meditation Practices

Formal meditation involves setting aside time for yourself each day to practice. Five basic meditations are described here. There are many other styles of meditation out there, so what's most important is finding one that feels comfortable to you. I recommend learning how to do at least one style of breath-based meditation, as that is something you can do anywhere, anytime. The following descriptions should be enough to get you started, but if you'd like more guidance or instruction, the resources section lists a number of books, websites, and apps.

Here are a few things to keep in mind as you read this section:

- Start out by meditating for about ten minutes each day. If that feels too long, start with five minutes or even two minutes. Consistency each day is the most important factor, so if you can do five minutes a day, that's better than twenty minutes once a week. Mindfulness is like a muscle, and each time we meditate, we are strengthening that muscle. The longer you meditate, the faster and more easily you will be able to get into a mindful mindset when you really need to.

- The best time of day to meditate will depend on you and your schedule. Some folks prefer to meditate in the morning when they've just woken up, to have a good start to the day, and others prefer clearing their minds at night before going to sleep. You're probably a busy parent with a lot going on, so my recommendation is to do it whenever you can. Early in the morning or in the evening after the kids are in bed are certainly both good choices. I try to get to my daughter's school about ten minutes early for pickup when I can, and I use that time to sit in the car and do a breathing or listening meditation. Sometimes I meditate while waiting at the doctor's office or in line at the grocery store or while I'm walking to work. There are no rules for this, so get creative and do what works for you.

- There is no such thing as a bad meditation session. As you meditate more, you will notice that there are times when your mind feels calm and steady and you are able to hold your attention with relative ease. There will be other days when your mind feels like a fish flopping out of water, and no matter how hard you try to get a hold on it, it keeps slipping through your fingers. In those situations, the best you can do is to loosen your grasp, let go of the thoughts, and keep coming back to your breathing, listening, or walking. If you have to do it every two seconds, that's okay. Hang in there. Even if you don't feel like you're seeing the benefits in your meditation session, you will see them in your daily life.

- If you miss a day or two or twelve, don't worry about it. There's no reason to stress out or feel guilty about it. Finding time to meditate when you have young children in the home can be especially challenging. As one of my mindfulness teachers once said to me, "Your children are your practice." So cut yourself some slack, and remember that no matter how long it's been, you can always, always begin again.

The four traditional ways to meditate are sitting down, standing, lying down, and walking. You can meditate with your eyes open or closed. Try a few different styles, and see what works for you. Different practices may work better depending on how you are feeling or on the time of day.

BREATHING

Get into a comfortable, alert position, either sitting or lying down. You can close your eyes or keep them open. Take a few deep, full breaths, and then let your breathing settle into its natural rhythm. Notice where your breath feels most obvious; perhaps it's at the tip of your nostrils, inside your nose, in the rising and falling of your chest, or in the expanding and contracting of your belly. Focus your attention on that spot. You don't have to change your breathing, but just pay attention to it. Whenever your mind wanders, as it will within a breath or two, gently bring it back. If you're having a hard time staying focused, you can either softly say "inhale" and "exhale" to yourself or count your breaths up to ten and then start again.

LISTENING

Get into a comfortable, alert position, either sitting or lying down. You can close your eyes or keep them open. Take a few deep, full breaths, and then just listen. Focus your attention on the sounds around you, whether it's your child's voice, your own breath moving in and out of your body, ambient sounds, or traffic whizzing by. When your attention wanders and you start thinking, just notice your thoughts, let them go, and come back to listening. Your attention will wander again, and when it does, just come back to listening again, and again. Remember, it's not about listening perfectly the whole time. It's about noticing when you have stopped listening and making the choice to bring your attention back to the sounds around you.

WALKING

Walking meditations are great for when your body just won't stop moving, when staying still for too long puts you to sleep, or when you need to be walking anyway, perhaps with a baby in a stroller or to get the dog out of the house. There are many ways to do this. Once again, it's about choosing something to pay attention to and then bringing your attention back to it again and again. You can do a listening or breathing meditation while walking, or you can count your steps up to ten and then start again. Alternately, you can choose to focus specifically on the act of walking itself, noticing the motions involved in taking each step. You may notice how you shift your weight from one foot to the other, lift your other foot, and then put it down. You can say to yourself, *Shift, lift, and step,* to help you stay focused. When your mind wanders, every few steps, just notice that it has wandered and bring it back to your listening, breathing, counting, or walking.

QUICK BODY SCAN

You can do this practice while sitting, standing, or lying down. The point here is to take a quick scan of your entire body to figure out where you may be holding tension or experiencing pain. It's not necessarily about relaxing or ending either sensation; it's more about becoming aware of what is going on in your body and how that may be impacting your thoughts, feelings, and interactions with others.

- Take a moment to get grounded. Notice the places where your body is coming into contact with the ground or your chair.

- Take three mindful breaths, noticing the air moving past your nose, the expansion of your chest, or the rising of your belly.

- Start with either your head or your feet (you can try both ways and see which one you prefer) and move your attention down or up through every part of your body, noticing if you are relaxed, in pain, tense, neutral, or something else altogether. If you start with your head, for example, you will want to scan your attention from your head and face down to your neck and shoulders and down each arm and into your fingers. From there, you can pay attention to your chest, belly, and back, and then your hips, pelvis, thighs, calves, ankles, and feet. If you don't feel anything in a certain part of your body, or you can't quite put words to what you are feeling, that's okay. It's just about noticing.

- As your mind wanders, which it will, notice the wandering and then bring your attention back to your body.

You may choose to try to relax tense muscles when you feel them, do some stretches, or give yourself a gentle massage, but the main point of this practice is to increase your self-awareness, so you can come to notice how and where your body holds your feelings and how those feelings may impact your behavior, and vice versa.

You can do this body scan in five minutes or in forty-five minutes, depending on how long you focus your attention on each part of your body. If you're having a hard time figuring out how to do it, there are a number of guided meditations available for free online.

LOVING-KINDNESS PRACTICE

Metta, or loving-kindness practice, is a type of meditation in which we intentionally think kind and loving thoughts toward ourselves and others with the intention of training our brains to do so more readily and easily. This goes along with the theory that neurons that fire together wire together. The more often we think or do something, the more likely we are to think or do that same thing again. It's easier to be patient and kind with our children when we've been practicing kindness all along.

The practice itself is quite simple, and you can do it while sitting, standing, walking, or even waiting in line at the store. Choose a person to be the focus of your attention (this could be yourself, someone you know and love, a neutral person such as your mail carrier, or the entire world) and repeat these phrases in your mind as you think of that person or persons:

May you be happy.

May you be healthy.

May you be safe.

May you live with ease.

Another variation that I like to use is *May you feel loved.* The words don't matter as much as the intention, so if these particular phrases don't work for you, you can pick any three or four phrases that you like.

Keep repeating the phrases for several minutes until you are ready to move to another person or group of people. (Traditionally, metta practice is directed first toward ourselves, then neutral individuals, then people who are causing us some difficulty, then the whole world. You can do this, or just choose one person to focus on.) When you notice your mind wandering, as it will, gently bring it back to the person you were thinking about and keep repeating the phrases.

Informal Practices

If formal meditation practice is like going to the gym for a serious workout several times each week (or even every day), then practicing informal mindfulness is akin to taking the stairs instead of the elevator, parking at the opposite end of the parking lot, or standing up from your desk chair to stretch for a few minutes. The point is to work mindfulness into your day. Anything you do in the course of a day represents an opportunity to practice paying attention with kindness and curiosity, from brushing your teeth in the morning to drinking your coffee or tea to sending an email, eating dinner with your family, or reading to your child. The goal here is not to pay attention perfectly but to set an intention to pay as much attention as you can to whatever you are doing without judging it or wishing it were different. As with meditation, your mind will wander, and your job is to notice the wandering and bring it back, again and again.

I recommend choosing one or two pleasant activities you do every day as a place to start. I try to pay attention when I'm showering (I can't tell you how many times I've gotten to the end of my shower and realized that my hair is wet but I have no idea if I actually remembered to wash it or not) and when I'm reading to my daughters. It wasn't until I started practicing mindfulness that I realized that I could get to the end of the book and have absolutely no idea what the story was about. My body was sitting on the couch, my eyes were scanning over the pages, and my voice was saying the words, but my mind was bouncing around among task lists, a worrisome conversation I'd had with a friend, a sick family member, my career plans, and that yoga class I forgot to get to. Once I started noticing when my mind was wandering and purposefully bringing it back to the book and my daughters, I found myself enjoying the experience of reading to them so much more. It no longer felt like a chore or something to get through, as it became an opportunity to connect with my daughters. More often than not, I came away feeling more relaxed and energized and happier.

Sarah Rudell Beach, mother of two young children and author of the blog *Left Brain Buddha* (2014), offers these opportunities for practicing mindfulness throughout the day, all of which are quite doable for busy parents:

- Awareness of routine activities, such as getting dressed, sitting in traffic, or waiting in line
- Awareness of technology, such as taking three deep breaths before sending an e-mail or answering your phone
- Interactions with your child or others, including listening carefully, paying attention to the games you are playing with them, or staying calm when they are having a hard time

- Cleaning or doing chores, such as vacuuming, folding laundry, or doing dishes
- Checking in with your body, perhaps by doing a brief body scan to discover where you might be holding tension, so you can choose to breathe for a minute and perhaps relax a bit. (See the CALM practice in chapter 1.)

Although any moment of the day represents an opportunity for mindfulness practice, please don't set a goal of trying to be mindful at every moment. This is surely a setup for failure, even if you happen to be raising children in a Zen monastery. Remember when you can, and be kind and forgiving to yourself when you realize you have forgotten.

Try This: Practice During the Three Ts

I love the suggestion from Meena Srinivasan (2014) to practice during the three Ts: tea time, transitional time, and toilet time. It can be hard for busy parents to remember to take a few moments to breathe during the day, but even short mindfulness breaks several times each day can result in significant reductions in stress. So each time you take a sip of tea (or coffee), go to the bathroom, or find yourself waiting in line or heading out the door, use those brief bits of time to breathe and reconnect with your body, your experience, and the present moment.

As you begin your mindfulness practice, I want you to keep two things in mind. First, it's so easy to get wrapped up in the details of mindfulness and what it is exactly and how to do it just the right way. Don't worry about that. If you remember nothing else, just remember to notice that your mind has wandered and breathe your way back to the present moment. If you can do that, you'll be fine. The second thing to remember is that mindfulness practice shouldn't be yet another thing to add to your endless task list. It's not about beating yourself up for spacing out, forgetting, or getting caught up in a totally mindless moment. The minute you do that, you're getting hijacked by that crazy monkey in your mind. Mindfulness is fundamentally about adopting an aware and compassionate approach to your own experience and that of others. Try not to get too frustrated with yourself when you miss the mark, because you will. We all do, over and over again, until we realize what's happening, which gives us an opportunity to make a different choice.

Sharing Your Practice with Your Child

As you begin to integrate formal and informal mindfulness practices into your daily life, you may want to share your experience with your child. You can do this in some very basic and straightforward ways: by showing her what you're doing, talking about it, and explaining how mindfulness impacts your thoughts, feelings, and behaviors. As mindfulness is fundamentally about your attitude and internal experience, your child may not make the connections between mindfulness and happiness, gratitude, compassion, and patience unless you find ways to tell her what you are doing and why you are doing it. The goal here is to be transparent about this aspect of your life without proselytizing or pushing it, so be sure to pay attention to how your child is responding. If she's not interested, let it go. You can always come back to it later.

Sharing your practice may require you to be vulnerable and open in ways that you are not entirely used to or comfortable with. The thing is, mindfulness isn't just about noticing when we're trying to do too much at once or when we've gotten so caught up in our own crazy thoughts that we've lost touch with reality; it's also about responding to ourselves with forgiveness and compassion each time that happens. It's about allowing ourselves to fully enjoy a beautiful moment without being overcome by nostalgia or anxiety, or to manage a difficult moment without reacting impulsively or unkindly. These are incredibly valuable lessons to share with our children, but if they are going to learn them, they need to see us live it and hear us talk about it. It can be easy to forget to talk to our children about it, and talking about it can be difficult to do, even when we do remember. I don't know about you, but I'm not chomping at the bit to tell my kids about all the ways I get distracted or confused or overly anxious; it's hard enough for me to admit it to myself. But each time we can own and share our experience in authentic and transparent ways, it will become an increasingly interesting and accessible option for our children, and they will be more likely to become interested in the mindfulness activities we offer them.

The parents I interviewed described a number of different ways to model and share mindful moments with children:

- Ask yourself questions out loud. This is a great way to model the curious interest that is central to mindfulness practice. Some examples are "What am I feeling?" "What am I thinking?" "What do I need right now?" "What can I do to be kind to myself or my kids?"

- Demonstrate compassion by handing granola bars or money to homeless people or by carrying a bug out of your house instead of killing it.

- Explain why you're not watching TV or reading a magazine during dinner. It can be tempting to say something like, "Because it's dinnertime," but when we talk about the value of being present and focused on our meals and each other, our children might learn something important about connection, ritual, and mindful eating.
- Appreciate joyful situations out loud. Don't be afraid to talk about how hard it can be to pay attention or stay connected, even in good times. Explain what it means to savor something, to fully immerse ourselves in an experience, and how doing so makes it more likely that we will fully experience and remember those moments and be changed by them.
- Be grateful out loud. The mere act of experiencing and expressing gratitude can transform almost any experience. As long as we are breathing, we have something to be grateful for, and remembering that truth can provide us with just enough perspective to get into a clearer and kinder head space.
- Let your child know why you are taking deep breaths and how it helps you manage a difficult situation.
- Describe a time when you made a mistake and were able to feel compassion and forgiveness for yourself.
- Talk about a meditation group, lecture, or book you've been enjoying.
- Listen to short meditations with your child. One mother noted that her children were especially responsive to this when they could choose the meditations off an app (see resources for suggestions).

- Engage in regular traditions and family rituals that can help bring you out of whatever rut you might be in and help all of you feel connected to each other, to your culture or heritage, and to the present moment.
- Put down your cell phone in an explicit, thoughtful way, such as designating a space near the entrance to the house where you leave it each day when you come in the door from work.
- Invite your child to join you as you meditate or practice yoga. Be sure to keep your expectations reasonable.
- If you use a meditation cushion or a singing bowl (a bell in the shape of a bowl that is struck with a small padded mallet and commonly used in meditation practices), leave them out so that your child can see them and play with them. If your child asks about what you're doing, talk to her about your experience.
- Remind yourself, out loud, that you can always, always begin again.

Those are a few ideas to get you started. Remember that the goal is to plant the seeds of mindfulness by sharing your own struggle and experience without any expectations about what your child will learn from it or do with it.

Try This: Practice Anyway

Although it's nice to practice meditation in quieter moments, it's not often that we parents have an extended period of stillness to ourselves. Learning to practice mindfulness even as life swirls around you is an incredibly valuable skill—in fact, it is the end goal of all this, as chaotic moments are when we most benefit from our practice. If you didn't get around to meditating before your kid woke up, try doing it afterward. Let her know what you are going to do, and invite her to join you—or crawl all over you, as the case may be. You can choose to practice a breathing or listening meditation, and each time you are distracted by whatever else is going on, come back to your breath or the sounds around you. Even if this practice lasts only two minutes, it is still a valuable learning experience for your child and a useful way to support your meditation habit.

John Teasdale, one of the leading researchers in the mindfulness community, notes that practicing mindfulness isn't difficult, but remembering to practice is (Borchard 2013). So treat yourself as you would hope to treat your child when she loses her focus or forgets something or gets carried away in a daydream—with kindness, acceptance, and gentle reminders to keep coming back to the present moment. The more you are able to do this, the more you will find yourself coming back to a mindful awareness throughout the day. As you have those experiences, find ways to share them with your child whenever you can. Each time you do so, you're setting the stage for her to join you on this journey. The next chapter will help you explore just how to share that journey with your child.

PART 2

Sharing Mindfulness With Your Child

CHAPTER 3

Helping Your Child Find His Inner Zen Master

It has been said that children are like little Zen masters. The first time I heard this, I almost spit out my coffee. My girls often seem more like My Little Ponies hopped up on too many lattes than serene spiritual leaders. Yet as I started to understand mindfulness and the process of tuning into my experience with kindness and curiosity—of finding an internal source of peace and stability amidst the endless chaos of life—I came to realize that my girls have the ability both to be deeply mindful and, in their less mindful moments, to challenge me to do the same. Jon Kabat-Zinn described it beautifully when he noted that "A Zen master is likely to continually push your buttons, so you have plenty of occasions to practice maintaining clarity and emotional balance. Children, by their very nature, are going to call into question and disrupt everything you know, and that is a great opportunity for bringing mindful awareness to the situation" (Kailus 2014). Modeling an attitude of acceptance, curiosity, and kindness is a highly effective way to teach these skills to our kids. Recognizing when our children are already doing it on their own and supporting them in those moments is another important way to help them develop a mindful mind-set. This chapter will talk about both of these practices in more detail. But first, here is an example of how children can be their own Zen masters.

My daughter recently started kindergarten in a bilingual immersion school. Two of her teachers would not be speaking English to her, and when she realized that she wouldn't be able to understand them, she started to panic. She spent the week leading up to her first day of school worrying and crying about it and telling us that she didn't want to go to kindergarten. I understood my daughter's concerns. Starting a new school is scary enough without the added stressor of an unknown language. Needless to say, drop-off on the first day wasn't pretty. She clung to me tearfully when I tried to leave. When I picked her up that afternoon, however, she jumped into my arms and asked if she could stay for the afternoon program and return the next day. Later that evening, I asked about her teachers who won't speak English to her. She paused briefly and then said, "Well, I guess I'd better figure out what they're saying. I'm trying to pay attention and look for clues."

My daughter had no idea, but in that moment, she was taking a mindful approach to the situation. It didn't involve a breathing exercise or any sort of guided activity, and I didn't have anything to do with it. Even so, she demonstrated two of the core practices of mindfulness: acceptance and curiosity. She stopped fighting her new reality and came to terms with the fact that she was going to this school and that her teachers were going to speak another language to her. From there, she was able to choose her behavior, and she decided she was going to be interested in what they were saying. My role in that situation was to support my daughter and get curious about her experience. I did this by listening carefully and asking her what kind of clues she might look for.

Try This: Ten Mindful Minutes

Set aside ten minutes to be mindful with your child. This may work best when your little one is immersed in play, but it can be anytime. Just be with him. Don't ask what he is doing, judge it, or make suggestions. Just notice your own experience and your child's. When you find your mind wandering to a dishwasher that needs to be emptied, a phone call that you need to make, or a show that you're aching to watch, notice those roving thoughts and then bring your attention back to your child. Notice what happens and how you feel each time you do this.

Encouraging Mindful Moments

I'm sure you've witnessed your child having a mindful moment. Perhaps it's when he is intent on building the tallest Lego tower ever or is spinning an elaborate tale about fairies living in the bedside table or is focused on hearing every word and note of a favorite song. Maybe it's when he's in the zone on the soccer field, about to score a goal. While none of these may seem like particularly mindful moments, they are. When your child is focused on just one thing, and he's fully engaged and not judging himself or wishing something were different, he is practicing mindfulness, even though he's not sitting cross-legged on the floor with his eyes closed. When your child is expressing interest in the world around him, by mushing his banana between his fingers to see what it feels like or by stopping to notice a flower growing through a crack in the pavement or by asking questions about what happens when we die, why we have to eat vegetables, or the shape of the human body, he is being mindfully curious about the world around him. And finally, when your child is aware of and concerned about someone else's feelings or health or well-being—when he brings a special toy to a crying sibling or makes a card for a friend's birthday or visits a sick friend after school—he's practicing mindful compassion.

These moments are important for several reasons. Each time our children are concentrating, being curious or creative, or demonstrating compassion, they are learning to pay attention and notice what is happening within them and around them. They are learning to make connections, think in new ways, and respond skillfully to difficult, challenging, or boring situations. They are practicing empathy and kindness toward themselves and others. And they are drawing on their own inner experience for inspiration, guidance, and soothing rather than counting on someone else to do it for them. The more often they do all of these things, the more likely they will be able to do them in the future, because even these seemingly small behaviors are developing and strengthening habits and skills and the neural connections in the relevant parts of their brains.

Those are just a few of the reasons why it's important to practice mindfulness with our children when they're calm, happy, and doing well. The other reason is that those are the times when they're most likely to be receptive to what we're trying to teach them. The more they practice these skills when they are in a good space, the more likely they'll be able to access and utilize them in difficult moments. As one of my mindfulness teachers once put it, "You can't practice crisis meditation."

As our children get better at practicing mindfulness in the calm, uneventful moments of daily life, the more likely they'll be able to access this skill when we really want them to—when they're overcome with anger, anxiety, or sadness. Actively teaching your child about the ideas and practices of mindfulness is part of that process, to be sure, and this will be covered more in later chapters. However, you'll be most successful in your endeavors if you can notice when your child is already being his own little Zen master and support him in that process or, at the very least, not get in his way.

This sounds fairly simple, and it is, but it's not necessarily easy, as children often choose to immerse themselves in this moment precisely when we want them to focus on the next one—which generally involves something like setting the table or getting out the door. Or their curiosity makes us uncomfortable, especially when they're asking about God or sex or the little purple lines on the back of our thighs that we'd much rather not talk about, thank you very much. If we miss those moments or don't realize how important they can be, or we just don't have the energy for a tough discussion, we're likely to blow right past them and yank our kids right along with us. As the father of two young children wrote so eloquently, "So, our job as parents seems to be to expunge this righteous 'nowness' like a stain; to make them understand the regret of past indiscretions and the pressure of future deadlines; to instill in them a sense of haste and forward motion; to teach them to wave farewell to 'the now' as they race off to 'the somewhere else.' We basically beat this 'living in the now' skill out of them until they turn into frustrated adults, who then spend a fortune on self-help books trying to find it again, which seems kind of absurd" (Chai 2012).

Now I'm not saying we should forgo errands and chores and homework and generally getting out the door and on with our lives just because our kids are busy making a Lego pirate ship or a glittery Valentine or because they're curious about how helicopters fly or why Mommy and Daddy aren't married to each other anymore. It's our job to teach our children how to get to places on time, transition between activities as smoothly as possible, and respond to requests from others, even when it's inconvenient or annoying to them. The thing is, that sort of learning is woven into the rhythm of our daily lives, and such moments are also opportunities for our children to practice acceptance of what is happening (such as Mommy asking you to put on your shoes) and to choose their own behavior from that place of acceptance ("Please, please choose to put on your shoes, child!"). However, as so many of us know all too well, the constant motion from this to that, the constant push to get things done, seems to happen whether we want it to or not; we rarely need to remind ourselves to feel stressed and hurried through the day. But we do need to remind ourselves, and our children, to slow down, pay attention, and get interested in the world around us. That's just one reason why a daily mindfulness practice can be so important.

When Your Child Is in a Mindful Mind-Set

Although any activity, from cleaning up to brushing teeth, is an opportunity for intentional awareness, there are five specific practices, five ways of being in the world, that are fundamental to mindfulness practice. It's not always easy to tell if your child is being mindful, but there are five related questions that you can ask yourself, in a sort of mini-assessment of the situation, to figure out whether your child is practicing mindfulness:

1. Is your child concentrating on just one thing?
2. Is he being creative, either in the activity he is doing or in the way he is thinking about a situation or solving a problem?

3. Is he being curious, perhaps about his own experience, a difficult situation, or someone else's perspective?

4. Is your child being compassionate toward either himself or anyone else, including animals or other living beings?

5. Is your child being quiet? This can be a tricky one—as some children are naturally quieter than others, and it's possible for a child to be sitting quietly and stewing—but it's often a good place to start.

So look for these experiences—concentration, creativity, curiosity, compassion, and silence—because each is a decent clue that your child is having a mindful moment. One important note: none of this counts if your child is staring at a television, tablet, or smartphone. Your kid may seem quiet and focused when he's watching a show, but the reality is that he's zoned out when staring at a screen. He's not engaged with his own experience in a thoughtful way.

Concentration

Concentration, or the ability to sustain attention, is a fundamental mindfulness skill—not to mention something that most parents wish their children had more of. It is also a practice, in the sense that the more we do it, the better we get at it. It doesn't necessarily have to be about thinking hard or working hard to figure something out; it's about keeping the focus of your attention on just one thing, whatever it may be, and noticing when your mind has wandered so you can choose to bring it back. Needless to say, this skill is not only incredibly valuable in the classroom, the recital hall, and the sports field but also crucial in times of intense emotion. More often than not, we tend to brush past, ignore, or distract ourselves away from difficult feelings, including anger, sadness, worry, and boredom—all of which can come up at any moment, whether it's at school, practice, or the dinner table. Each time we can teach our children to pay attention to those unpleasant feelings, they will experience the paradoxically healing power of actually feeling their feelings rather than trying to escape from them, and they'll learn that feelings are just feelings—not reality—and they won't last forever. The best way to do this is to start by noticing when your child is actually concentrating and to not get in his way. If he's having a hard time staying with a difficult experience, you can best support him in his endeavor by responding with curiosity and compassion.

Try This: Concentration Games

There are several games and activities to help children build concentration skills, including memory games, puzzles, Jenga, hidden pictures (where you search for hidden items in a larger picture or for something that's wrong with a picture), or craft projects such as knitting or coloring mandalas—patterns that often have circular designs and many different repetitive shapes in them.

Creativity

Although being creative isn't in the formal definition of mindfulness, it is relevant and such a part of the childhood experience that it's worth including. I see this in my older daughter, who loves to draw. She works hard on her drawings, making detailed pictures of just about anything that comes to mind: children playing, fairies flying, animal parades, and even her own dreams at night. My daughter has fairly decent art skills for a five-year-old, but she's still just a five-year-old. Yet she has never once told me that she can't draw something—she just doesn't have a perfectionist voice in her head telling her that she doesn't know how to draw something or that she's not good enough. She puts pen to paper and does the best she can. This is mindfulness in action.

Not surprisingly, my daughter's drawings often reflect something she is struggling with or trying to communicate. I remember one time when she was about three years old and she got really angry with me over something. She took out a fat gray marker and scribbled angrily all over a large piece of white paper. This incident illustrated to me how the creativity of children can provide a window into their inner world, which can help us parents understand them a bit better, so we can know how to engage with them about what they're feeling and thinking.

Each time my daughters draw or engage in any other creative endeavor, they are setting the stage for several factors that are directly relevant to the mindful experience. First, they are generally concentrating on just one thing, which is fundamental to mindfulness. Second, they are getting curious about something in their own experience or in the world around them. They are wondering what is possible, what they can create or make or imagine on their own, without the guidance or feedback of another. And finally, whether they realize it or not, they are treating themselves with compassion and kindness, both of which are necessary for the creative process to continue. Think about what happens when your child starts judging himself harshly or comparing his skills to someone else's. My guess is that, more often than not, he gives up.

Just to be clear, creativity isn't only about art or music or blocks, although it starts that way for many children. Creativity is also about a new way of thinking in the classroom or moving on the sports field or a different way of responding to a family member or a friend. However it manifests for our children, it's our job to notice when it is happening and to support the process.

Try This: Draw the Feeling

This is a great way to help your child begin to recognize and identify feelings. You can start by reading a book about different feelings and talking about them. From there, you can either give your child a piece of paper and some markers and ask him to draw different feelings or draw an outline of a body and ask your child to draw where the feelings live in his body and what they look like. Try not to judge or correct your child, and if you feel a need to ask questions about what he's drawing, saying "Can you tell me more about that?" is always a good place to start. As with so many of the activities listed in this book, this one will go more smoothly if you do it with your child.

Curiosity

"Why?" and "How do you know?" These are the two most common questions in my house these days, and—I won't lie—they often make me want to bang my head against the wall. While there may be times when my daughters ask these questions with the explicit goal of trying to defeat me, often they are genuinely curious. They want to know how the world works or why it doesn't, and how I have come to know what I know or why I don't.

As tired as I may be of answering questions, I try to take them seriously whenever possible, because curiosity is a powerful skill that I want my children to cultivate. It is an important part of the learning process, and an invaluable life skill. Curiosity is a desire to learn or know more about something or someone, which we can't have if we're using up all of our mental energy fighting or judging or wishing something were different. Any time your kid is being curious, it means that he has accepted whatever is going on and decided to get interested in it. From that place of wonder and openness, he is likely to learn something new about himself or others or the world around him. The best you can do in those moments is to get interested with him or, at the very least, not shut down his curiosity by giving him answers, telling him how to manage the situation, or doing things for him.

Try This: Ask Questions in the Hard Moments

Children often come to us parents with difficult or confusing situations that may not have clear solutions. Perhaps it's a tummy ache that won't go away, a friend who isn't playing nicely on the playground, or an inexplicable bout of sadness. Often our first impulse is to try to fix the problem. Sometimes we can, and that's great. But when we can't, curiosity is an empathic and effective way to respond. Asking open-ended questions about your child's experience and then hearing and accepting his answers, whatever they may be, lets him know that you care and that you won't be scared off by whatever he's struggling with, and it's a great way to model a curious and mindful approach to life. Also there's a bonus: you and your child may actually get some insight into what's going on and what to do next.

Compassion

It is possible, I suppose, for a child to be completely aware, focused, and intentional as he whacks his brother, but that's not mindfulness. Compassion, or connecting with the experience of someone who is suffering and wanting to support or help them, is a fundamental aspect of mindful awareness. We want our children to learn to slow down and come to a place of acceptance about whatever is happening so that they can move forward in a thoughtful, skillful, and compassionate way. That may mean gently shepherding a lost bug out the door, helping a sibling with difficult homework, making the choice to take care of themselves, or not hitting someone in the face, as Tyran Williams reminded us. It may also mean just thinking kind thoughts about another person and wishing them well.

How to teach your child the importance of kindness and how to practice more of it will be an ongoing topic in this book. For now, the thing to remember is to notice when your kid is taking care of others and of himself and to notice it with him. You don't have to make a big deal out of it or shower him with praise, but the act of noticing out loud powerfully reinforces this important way of being in the world.

Try This: We All Make Mistakes

One of the most powerful ways to cultivate compassion, both for ourselves and for others, is to remember that we're not alone in our imperfection. When something goes wrong—for either you or your child—try to share one of your mistakes with him in an honest and accepting way, and remind him that everyone makes mistakes. No one is perfect, and that's totally okay. This simple truth is so powerful and yet can be so hard to remember.

Quiet

"Do you want to listen to music?"

I ask this question of my daughters most days during our ride home from school. More often than not, they decline. They would prefer to sit quietly and stare out the window after a long day. This used to bother me: how will they ever learn to appreciate music if we don't listen to it enough? Over time, however, I came to appreciate and support their desire for a few moments of silence in the middle of a hectic day, as virtually nothing else about our lives is conducive to quiet reflection.

Silence is so important for children, both because of what happens when they can get and stay quiet and because of what happens when they can't. A constant stream of noise pulls their attention in different directions and distracts them from what is happening in their own bodies and minds. Too much noise can increase stress levels, even when they don't realize it. If our children are constantly listening to the voices of other people, they won't ever figure out what their own voice sounds like, what they truly think and want and need and what matters to them. And if they are constantly talking, constantly letting every thought that crosses their mind come out of their mouths, they'll likely miss out on the chance to evaluate their thoughts before they share them. One of the most powerful lessons we can teach our children is that our thoughts are just thoughts. They aren't reality, they aren't necessarily right, and we don't need to give them all equal airtime. A few moments of quiet contemplation often give us just enough time and space to notice our thoughts and figure out which ones are worth keeping and which ones aren't.

There's a reason why we tend to pray and meditate in silence: it helps us still our minds and bodies, so we can get to know ourselves a little bit better. A few moments of quiet can help your child get calm and grounded again in difficult times, if he is accustomed to it. But it isn't easy; the thoughts that arrive in those moments are often unpleasant or scary, and silence can be boring. All of these are reasons why we need to create opportunities for our children to experience silence and to not get in their way. This can be as challenging for us parents as it is for our children; I often find myself wanting to talk to my daughter in the car on the way to school or wanting to turn on the music as soon as we get home. The more we let our children be in silence, the more they will be able to be in silence, which is a skill that will serve them well throughout their lives.

Try This: Two-Minute Listening Meditation

It can be hard for children to be silent if they aren't used to it. Turning it into a game can help. Set a timer for one or two minutes and ask your kid to listen until the timer goes off. Let him know that he can report back to you on what he heard, if he wants to. For younger children, it may be helpful to be a bit more directive, such as by asking them to notice two or three sounds that they can then tell you about when the timer goes off.

How to Respond to Your Child's Mindful Moments

Perhaps by now I've convinced you that your kid is actually capable of accessing his inner Buddha from time to time. Once you realize what's happening, your job is to find ways to support him in his moments of Zen training, no matter how brief they may be. Doing this successfully is all about how you respond. Regardless of the situation, the best possible responses involve connecting, getting curious, or showing compassion. If you can't do any of those, or if none of those feels right in the moment, then you can just stay silent. If all of this seems a bit complicated for your addled, sleep-deprived parenting brain, here's the short version: *Notice and be nice, or get out of the way.* Seriously. There are times when I feel as though I should engage with my children, and yet for various reasons, I have neither the energy nor the desire. When that happens, the best I can do is to restrain myself from nagging, suggesting, critiquing, or complimenting—all of which are likely to distract my girls from whatever they are working on. The rest of the time, however, I try to create the time and space they need to be the Zen masters I know they can be, and then try to notice what they are doing, so I can respond as intentionally as possible with curiosity and compassion.

Connect

Here is a common scene in my morning routine: I tell my kids to get their shoes on. They're coloring or reading or playing—totally engrossed in their experience—so they don't hear me. Or they choose not to listen. I tell them again to get their shoes on, this time with a bit more tension in my voice. I head into the kitchen to finish making their lunches. I'm inevitably feeling stressed about getting to school on time, so I yell at them to get their shoes on, already. At least half the time, they're already doing it, and so they yell back at me. And then I yell at them to not yell at me, and in just a few short minutes, a relatively peaceful morning has spiraled into a screaming match over nothing. All because I didn't take two seconds to peek around the corner to see if the girls were doing what I had asked them to do.

Remembering to just connect with your child's experience can make all the difference in your interactions. Creating the time and space our children need to practice on their own is important, but we're unlikely to do this on a regular basis if we don't notice that our kids are having a mindful moment in the first place. For that to happen, we need to connect with our children's experience, which can mean taking a moment to notice or become aware of what they're thinking or feeling or doing. Focusing our awareness on our children long enough to see what is actually happening is our best shot at responding to them thoughtfully and intentionally. As with so many other mindfulness practices, it sounds ridiculously simple, and it is. Yet in the hustle of a busy day, as our attention is divided between our own thoughts and our interactions with our children, it can be hard to remember to do.

There are certainly going to be times—many of them each day, in fact—when we see what our kids are doing and we still need to nag them to get dressed or go to the bathroom or clean up their toys, or whatever it may be. Taking a moment to connect sounds like an obvious thing to do, and it is, and yet so many of us skip right past the connecting part as we rush along with the rest of our day. However, to the extent that we can slow down enough to see what our children are doing, remember why it matters, and acknowledge it with them before we move them on to the next thing, we're taking an important step in their mindfulness training as well as our own.

Try This: Take Two Breaths Before You Give Two Minutes

Most parents I know give their kids "two more minutes" before leaving a party or transitioning to a meal or to bedtime. Giving our kids a heads-up is a great idea, as it gives them a chance to finish whatever they're doing and to get ready mentally and physically for what's coming next. However, we parents often do this without noticing what is going on for our kids right then, and as a result, our interventions may not be as effective as they could be. So, next time you're ready to give the two-minute warning, take two mindful, intentional breaths first. Get yourself grounded, take a minute to really see what is happening for your kid, acknowledge it with him, and then let him know what's coming next.

Get Curious

Perhaps by now you're starting to connect with your child's experience so that you're noticing when he is concentrating, creating, being curious or compassionate, or just sitting in silence or playing quietly for a few moments. From there, the next three steps—getting curious, being compassionate, or staying silent yourself—are all about how to be with and respond to your child once you realize that he's in a mindful head space.

What I am suggesting is that you get mindful with your child. Connecting was the first step; that's all about noticing and accepting whatever is happening for him. From there, you can get curious, either in your mind or in the words you use with him, whatever seems appropriate for the moment. If he seems to be interested in discussing whatever is going on with you, you can respond by listening and asking questions, but if he's fully immersed in whatever he's doing, you may just want to notice and wonder about it quietly, so as not to disrupt his experience.

As a rule, I encourage you to ask open-ended questions that elicit creative answers rather than just yes or no questions. Younger children may benefit from more concrete and specific questions, such as "What are you building with those blocks?" while you may get more interesting answers from older children if you ask more general questions like "What are you up to?" or "Can you tell me more about it?" It can be useful to vary your questions. There's a reason why "How was school today?" usually elicits a response of "Fine." A fairly boring question is likely to get a fairly boring answer—especially when it's asked so often as to become meaningless.

If we parents can take a minute to figure out what we're really curious about, we're more likely to ask our children a range of interesting questions. For example, I don't actually want to know what my kid did at school that day (she played, she did an activity, she peed twenty-seven times, she ate half of her sandwich, most of which isn't terribly interesting to me). I want to know what she did that was new or challenging or interesting or really not fun at all. I want to know when she was nice to a friend, or vice versa, or if something happened that scared or excited her. And if that's what I want to know, it's what I need to find a way to ask about.

So, the next time you notice that you're curious about something going on with your child, share your interest with him in an interesting way. If you can't do that, because your brain is fried or you're too exhausted to be interested in anything, it's okay. Just get quiet and listen. Eventually he'll start talking or you'll get into a better head space to start asking.

Try This: Don't Ask Why

As mentioned before, "Why?" is a pretty common question in my house, and it's not only coming from my daughters. It's often tempting to ask why, as if figuring out the answer to that question will solve all the mysteries of virtually any situation. "Why?" can be a challenging question for children, however, especially in the aftermath of a particularly difficult event or experience. The reality is that, more often than not, children (and even adults) don't have a clear answer—we can't always explain our behavior, especially if we weren't in a particularly mindful head space at the time. Instead of asking why, try some of the following questions:

- "What happened?"
- "What did you do?"
- "How did you respond?"
- "How did you feel about it?"
- "What do you think about what happened?"

- "What did you notice in your body?"
- "What surprised you about what happened?"
- "What did you think worked well?"
- "What didn't work so well?"
- "What do you want to do the same next time?"
- "What do you want to do differently next time?"
- "What do you need from me?"
- "What can I do to help?"

When asking these questions, it's important to notice if you're hoping for or expecting a specific answer. If you are, your child will probably pick up on your expectations and either give you what you want to get you off his back, or disengage entirely. If you can let go of your desired response and get genuinely curious about your child's experience, you'll have a much more meaningful and honest interaction with him. And remember, mindful curiosity can happen out loud or through your silent presence.

Show Compassion

Compassion can feel like such a big concept, something that belongs in the world of the Dalai Lama or Mother Teresa, a practice that requires a pure heart and great wisdom. The good news is that it's really not that fancy, and we don't have to be saints to practice compassion on a regular basis or to experience its effects. It's just about remembering that we're all in this together. I'm talking about noticing when our children are suffering or struggling, and expressing concern or warmth or love or just being nice to them. This is not to say that compassion is always easy. Before I had children, I assumed that I would feel a constant stream of happy, positive thoughts toward my beloved child and nothing else. Ever.

As anyone who has been a parent for longer than about two days can tell you, raising children is exhausting and exasperating and boring and occasionally rage-inducing, and sometimes it is incredibly difficult to find a way into the feelings of love and kindness that we know we have for our children. This is never truer than in those moments when our children are in their own bad space. I know that when my daughters are really sad or angry, my gut reaction is to find a way to either make them feel better or get them to go away until they feel better, so I don't have to deal with their tough feelings. The thing is, I'm a grown-up with a fully functional prefrontal cortex and a lifetime of figuring out how to deal with unpleasant experiences. My daughters are little, their brains are still growing; they're still figuring all of this out, and they need my help to do so.

When your child is having a moment—either a mindful one or a difficult one—the most skillful and empathic choice you can make is to be kind. There are many, many ways to do this. It may be about sitting nearby with a calm, abiding presence. Or perhaps your child needs to be snuggled or tucked into a comfy spot with a favorite toy or blanket. Maybe he needs to hear a story about a time when you also made a bad mistake or got hurt by a friend or lost a beloved pet, so he doesn't feel so alone. Or maybe he needs to be reminded that, no matter how confusing or scary or out of control the world may feel, you're here and you're going to take care of him, and you're not leaving.

One note here: compassion is not the same as praise. Inherent in compassion is a sense of togetherness. The kindness of compassion says, "I understand what you're experiencing and I've felt it too, and it's okay, whatever it is." And sometimes it says, "I have no idea what you're thinking or what you're up to, but I'm interested in learning more, and I'm not afraid to stick around until we figure it out." Sometimes compassion can be as basic as "I love you, no matter what." Fundamentally, compassion is about truly being with your child's experience in a kind and curious way. Praise is a whole different ball game; praise is about passing judgment on whether or not your child has done a good job. It shifts from a focus on just being with your child to a focus on evaluating him, which can cause anxiety in both of you, even if you are trying to tell your child that he is doing a good job. This is exactly the opposite of the attitude of acceptance that you're trying to cultivate and share in these moments. Don't get me wrong; there is certainly a time and place to give your child positive feedback, but this isn't it.

Try This: Send a Little Love

Sometimes it may not be easy to be compassionate with your kid. Maybe he's being annoying, maybe it's been a hard day, maybe you're exhausted or frustrated or sad or angry. It happens to all of us. When that happens, try sending a little quiet love, as described in the loving-kindness practice in chapter 2. You can silently repeat phrases such as *May you be happy. May you feel loved.* If those specific words don't work for you, feel free to choose others. The goal here is not for your child to detect what you're thinking but rather for you to get into a better head- and heart-space. It might not work in that exact moment, but it will work over time.

Be Silent

I've said it before, and I'll say it again. Sometimes the best thing we can do to help our children cultivate their inner Buddhas is to notice and say nothing. Like mindfulness itself, this practice is simple but far from easy. Most of us are not used to moving through life quietly, and it's not even something that most parenting books recommend. From the moment our babies are born, we are encouraged to speak to them constantly, to read and sing to them, and to narrate our lives in their presence so that they will develop strong verbal skills. While some amount of talking and reading to our children is certainly important, it needs to be balanced with moments of silence, moments when we can simply be present with our children. Not saying anything can be useful, whether our kids are in a calm, focused place or if they're actively struggling with something and not giving up or getting frustrated.

A calm, quiet presence can be supportive, loving, and nonintrusive. Sometimes it also may be the best you can do. If you find yourself wanting to nag or suggest or critique or encourage, then it's better to breathe or go into the other room or stand on one foot or do whatever it takes to get quiet. This is not bad parenting, I promise. This is calm abiding, and sometimes it's exactly what our children need so they can get on with the important work they're doing at that moment, whatever it may be.

Try This: Remember Your Mantra

If you're anything like me, staying quiet isn't easy. When I notice an impulse to start talking or suggesting or encouraging, I try to remember a simple phrase I heard once, which has been attributed to Gandhi: "Speak only if it improves on the silence."

Repeating those words like a mantra reminds me to really pay attention to what's going on with my children and myself and to figure out whether my words can really improve on the current moment. More often than not, they can't. Feel free to use the words suggested here or to come up with your own words to use as a mantra when you would rather keep silent than speak.

As you have likely realized by now, practicing mindfulness isn't necessarily easy, nor is it easy to teach to our kids. Fortunately, we're not teaching it to newbies. Children come into this world with an amazing capacity to be fully present in the moment, to be immensely interested in what is going on around them and within them, and to care deeply for other people. Recognizing and honoring those moments when we actually have a baby Buddha sitting right in front of us is the first and most important step toward strengthening our kids' mindfulness skills. After all, it's much easier to build on a skill that already exists than to tear it down and start all over again. From there, we can create spaces and reminders in our home that will support our children in developing mindful awareness whenever possible. How to do that will be covered next, in chapter 4.

CHAPTER 4

Making Space in Your Lives for Mindfulness

As discussed in chapter 3, children are quite capable of living in the present moment. They get immersed in games and stories and drawings and train sets and sports and books. They are immensely curious about the world around them and capable of great kindness in ways that often surprise us. Our kids are likely to do all of this regardless of what we do, but over time the experiences and responsibilities of life—the schedules and homework and practices and chores and friendships and everything else—will eventually conspire to pull them into the future and the past, into the regrets, worries, and fears that form the landscape of most adult minds. It's not our job to shield our children from these realities or to fix it for them each time they appear, but we can give them the skills to manage it all as mindfully and effectively as possible.

The first step is to create and protect as many opportunities as we can for our children to get and stay present. We can do this by intentionally setting aside the time and space that will make it as likely as possible that our children will get into a mindful head space when they need to. The idea is to create a structure in the time and space of your lives that will give your child the mental, emotional, and physical space to get calm, centered, and focused on her own. This chapter will talk about just how to do that.

Creating the Time and Space for Mindfulness

There are three main ways to create the time and space our kids need: slowing down in our daily lives so we can be more responsive to our children's mindful moments, setting aside significant blocks of unstructured time for them to use as they wish, and creating spaces in our homes that are soothing and relaxing for them. This chapter will discuss each of these as well as how to set aside a specific place, or a calm-down corner, for children who may benefit from a little more physical space when they are dealing with spinning thoughts or big feelings.

Slow Down

Although any moment, no matter what they are doing, is an opportunity for our children to come back to the here and now and get centered and focused, the reality is that it's not possible for them to be constantly aware. Their brains are working too fast, they have too much to do, and they simply forget. However, weaving small moments of mindfulness into their daily lives can make a big difference. A brief pause to take a breath together and admire a sunset or a flower or a ladybug—or allowing our kids to struggle with their shoelaces, seat belts, or spelling words rather than stepping in and doing it for them—can give them just enough calm, perspective, and awareness to keep them moving through their day as skillfully as they possibly can.

Once we realize how important this is, we can choose to balance the moments of rushing and nudging and suggesting with moments when we can just let our children be, if only for a moment. Because it can be so hard to remember to take these mindful moments, it's helpful to build structure and reminders into your day. The structure may include starting transitions a few minutes earlier whenever possible so that you don't feel quite as rushed. You may choose to get into the habit of taking three mindful breaths with your child before you step out the door, whenever the phone rings, or when you sit down to a meal. Anything you do on a daily basis can be a trigger for a brief moment of awareness, and you can choose to slow down at any point. The trick is to get into the habit of remembering.

As with most of the activities in this book, your quest to slow down will be more effective if you talk to your child about what you're trying to do and why it matters. From there, you can ask for ideas and suggestions about how to find moments of calm throughout the day. Does your child want to wake up a few minutes earlier in the morning? Say a family blessing or gratitude before dinner? Have five minutes of quiet snuggling or breathing upon arriving home from school? Your kid will likely come up with ideas you hadn't thought of, and she'll be more likely to remember and help you remember, if she has some ownership over the process.

Try This: The Slow-Walking Game

As parents, it can seem like we are always nudging our children to hurry up, to move faster, because we've got to get going. The next time you find yourself with a little extra time, practice the slow-walking game. Pick a spot that you need to get to and see who can get there the slowest. The only rule is that everyone has to be moving the entire time. When the game is over, you might want to explore with your child what it was like to make a choice to move slowly. How did it feel? How was it different from the times when she was rushing?

Set Aside Free Time Every Day

It's hard to overstate how much children benefit from having time to play or explore or even be a little bored, without someone telling them what to do or reminding them of the rules or guiding them through an exercise. Children need time to get creative, get to know themselves and their own thoughts, and tackle problems on their own. For most children, this takes the form of play, but whatever it looks like (journaling, spacing out, or listening to music), it is a crucial part of their mindfulness training. Ideally, we would find a chunk of time every day to let this happen, but that's not always possible, and sometimes these moments are literally just moments. However, if you find that your child doesn't have regular periods of unstructured time because she has extracurricular activities every day of the week, I would strongly encourage you to forgo some of those practices or tutors. It's often effective to set aside unstructured time, as you would for any other lesson or appointment, so you don't have to think about it or plan ahead for it and so your child comes to expect it.

Try This: Free Play

This is essentially the same as saying to your child, "Go away and play by yourself," but how you say it can make all the difference.

When you frame unstructured time as free play, you are communicating to your child that this is different from directed play and that she has the power to choose what she wants to do. Kids love that. If your child is having a hard time getting into the free play idea, you can start her off by sitting down to play Legos or reading her a book or drawing with her, and once she gets in the zone, try to extract yourself as stealthily as possible.

As you start to integrate more unstructured time into your child's life, you may notice that she's not always sure what to do with herself. This is especially likely if her life has been highly scheduled. She may wander aimlessly, complain of being bored, and get easily frustrated. This may be a normal response to a change in routine, and it will get better. However, it also may have to do with the physical space your child is in. People of all ages benefit greatly from having an uncluttered place to go to when they need to calm down and get focused and centered.

Make a Place for Your Kid to Get Some Headspace

I have been on meditation retreats in several different locations; without exception, the meditation halls and bedrooms are clean, sparsely decorated, and uncluttered, and the buildings surrounded by expansive and welcoming fields and woods. This isn't a coincidence; these spaces are specifically designed to help retreat participants stay calm and focused. Unnecessary clutter, messy piles, and lots of visual stimulation can be distracting and stress inducing; it can leave us feeling stuck, overwhelmed, and unsure of what to do next to calm down and get centered. This is just the opposite of what we want for our children when they're having a hard time.

The reality is that most of us don't live in a Zen monastery or retreat center. If your house looks anything like mine, you've got piles of dishes, laundry, children's art, paperwork, Legos, toy cars, and fairy figurines scattered around, and it's probably not infrequent that you or your child loses something important, such as your car keys or Barbie's favorite dress. All of the clutter can make it hard for children to select and find the toys or activities they want to play with and to get and stay calm and focused on just one thing when they need to. Fortunately, you don't have to turn your house into a hermitage in order to make it more conducive to mindful living, but there are a few changes you may want to consider. Several options are suggested here. Please take the time to consider which ones resonate with the culture and style of your family.

DECLUTTER

This is a big step and an important one. To the extent that you can clean out and clear out the unnecessary stuff in your home, you will all have more mind and heart space for what truly matters: staying aware in the present moment with kindness and curiosity. There are many print and online resources about how to declutter your home (see resources). It is important to keep in mind that keeping your house free of unnecessary stuff is a two-step process: getting rid of items that no longer serve a purpose, and making a choice not to clutter up your house all over again. This means breaking a cycle of consumption, which isn't easy, but it's worth it.

Because this book is about helping our children get calm and focused, your child's toys can be a great place to start. Kids who have too many toys will be distracted and overwhelmed by them, and it's hard to play well with any one toy when it's buried at the bottom of a pile. In addition, if your child has too many toys, she may never learn to be bored, which is a crucial experience that every child needs to have, again and again. The ability to tolerate boredom gives children the opportunity to recognize their own emotions and internal landscape and realize how to deal with it. It fosters creativity, resourcefulness, and resilience, and as anyone who has ever stood in a long line or waited for a doctor who's running late can tell you, it's an incredibly valuable life skill to have.

If your child is young enough, you can sort through her toys on your own (and in fact, I'd recommend it—otherwise you'll never get rid of anything), but be sure not to toss anything truly beloved. As children get older, it's important to involve them in the process. They may be more likely to buy into the plan if you clearly describe your reasons, and if they know you are also decluttering your own belongings.

The authors of *Simplicity Parenting*, Kim John Payne and Lisa Ross (2010), offer a number of useful suggestions for deciding which toys to get rid of:

- Broken toys or toys that are missing important pieces
- Toys that you have several of, when only one or two are required
- Developmentally inappropriate toys (toys that children have outgrown)
- Toys that do too much or break too easily
- High-stimulation toys (toys with lots of lights and sounds, for example)

- Annoying or offensive toys (you get to make this call)
- Toys that inspire corrosive play (guns, swords, and so on)

If you're not sure whether to keep something, or if you and your child disagree about a particular item, you can always put it in a box and stick it in the basement or the attic. If both of you forget about it, that's probably a good indication that you can get it out of the house once and for all. Just be sure to write a date on the box, so you'll know how long it's been untouched.

CHOOSE TOYS CAREFULLY

Culling useless, unnecessary, or unhelpful toys is a great first step toward creating a more mindful play space for your child. Making sure she has access to a range of toys that will help her practice the skills that you want her to have, such as focus, concentration, and creativity, is the next step. Payne and Ross (2010) offer some good suggestions, depending on your child's age and interests:

- Building toys, such as wooden blocks, magnetic blocks or tiles, train or race-car tracks
- Legos or Erector sets
- Toy cars and trucks, dolls, dollhouse
- Small animal or people figurines (preferably not branded, since children are more creative without a premade story in mind)
- Dress-up clothes and pieces of fabric
- Puzzles, dominoes, card games, and board games
- Empty cardboard boxes or shoeboxes of different sizes

- Craft supplies, including white and colored paper, markers, crayons, glue, scissors, tape, yarn, glitter, beads, buttons, and Play-Doh
- Origami paper and instructions
- Books and journals
- Workbooks with mazes, crossword puzzles, logic games, and so on

If you don't have a great surface for craft projects, try covering a table in your house with an oilcloth tablecloth. Our dining room is permanently covered with one, and we can easily wipe off markers or clean away Play-Doh. The same surface can be used for board or card games, jigsaw puzzles, and other activities.

Finally, your child needs time outside too. Many parents I know worry about having "good enough" outdoor space for their children to play in. As long as they're safe, any outdoor space is great. Balls, shovels, and buckets are inexpensive and useful toys, but you'd be amazed at how well kids can do with dirt, sticks, and rocks, too. Fresh air and room to move their bodies can keep children occupied for hours of mindful play.

USE VISUAL REMINDERS TO SLOW DOWN AND GET PRESENT

Thoughtfully chosen photographs and artwork—or even little sticky notes, drawings, or lists made by your child and placed carefully throughout your home—can be a fun and useful way to help everyone in the family remember to take a deep breath and notice what is happening right now, without judging it or wishing it were different, so they can make a better choice. You can choose visual reminders that make sense to you, and when your child is old enough, you can ask for her suggestions.

The goal here is to create a space that is as conducive to mindfulness as possible, because the more often you can remember to breathe, go slowly, and do just one thing at a time, the more likely your child will be able to do the same thing. Here are a few options to consider:

- Photographs or paintings of images that are especially meaningful or grounding
- Religious or spiritual artwork or iconography
- Pictures of loved ones or special family moments
- Artwork, drawings, or notes that say "Breathe" or "STOP" (see chapter 1 for the STOP exercise)
- A mindfulness bell that your child can ring when she needs an auditory cue to help her calm down (you may want to wait until your child is old enough to use the bell thoughtfully; otherwise the constant banging and ringing might have the opposite effect of what you were hoping for)
- Plants or flowers (fresh or dried or even plastic flowers can have a lovely effect)
- A nature centerpiece (for your kitchen or dining room table, decorated with items your child finds outside, such as rocks, flowers, feathers, pinecones, and leaves, as a reminder to slow down and reconnect with the changing seasons)
- Dream catchers on the wall above your child's bed
- Dream jar for collecting dreams (see the next exercise)
- Appreciation jar with a small basket of paper and pencils nearby (see the next exercise)

Try This: Make a Dream or Appreciation Jar

Fill an empty jar with colorful slips of paper that contain ideas for dreams, such as playing with big colorful balloons, picking flowers in a field, running a race around a track, eating popcorn at your favorite movie, eating a giant peach pie, or whatever comes to mind. Each night before bedtime, your child can choose a dream, or at the very least, a lovely thought to ponder as she falls asleep.

Similarly, you can make an appreciation jar or make one for each person in the house. Each time someone in your family appreciates or feels gratitude for another family member, they can write about it on a slip of paper and put it in the appreciation jar. This is a great way to practice kindness and feel connected to each other. Once a week or once a month, you can all read through the slips of paper in the jar.

It's also useful to have reminders or drawings up on display that will help your child remember what to do when she feels overwhelmed. You can work together to make a list of activities that she can try when she's having trouble dealing with big feelings, including anger, sadness, or worry. Have her draw pictures or write out the words, depending on her preference. Some ideas are dancing, drawing, running outside, breathing, looking at books, listening to music, snuggling, and stretching. Whatever works for you and your child is fair game (as long as it isn't violent or aggressive, of course). You'll want to hang the list on the fridge or anywhere your child can easily see it.

Try This: Get Outside to Go Inside

Many books and articles about mindful parenting talk about spending time outdoors. While it is true that the only Zen we will find in our backyard or at the local park is the Zen we bring there, the reality is that children tend to be calmer, happier, and more focused when they're playing outside. And while a beach vacation or beautiful vista is always lovely, any outdoor space can be a great opportunity for your child to move her body, breathe deeply, or just sit quietly. Kids may be more likely to get a little space from whatever difficult thoughts or feelings they may be struggling with and to come back to the experience of the present moment when they get outside.

Creating a Calm-Down Corner

In addition to making a more mindful environment throughout your house, you may want to consider creating a special calm-down corner. This can be a small room or even a corner of a room, a small comfortable chair, or an indoor child's tent. The idea is to create a space that is conducive to a calm, mindful experience and that specifically cues your child to get quiet and focused. It's a good idea to involve your child as much as possible in the design of this space and in choosing what to put in it. You'll want it to be decorated in a way that appeals to her, keeps her interested, and helps her get and stay calm. Here are a few other things to have in mind:

- You can choose a calming theme for the space, but you don't have to. I have one friend who named her kid's space the "Cool-Down Corner" and filled it with books about Antarctica as well as a few stuffed polar bears and penguins. Another friend created a "Seat in Space." She and her son cut out some stars and planets to hang from the sky, and included a favorite stuffed alien doll and a few different space-themed toys and books.

- Choose a few toys that your child would like to have or activities that she can do completely unsupervised (see suggestions in the next section). You'll want to work with her to choose things that are age or developmentally appropriate.
- Don't put too much stuff in the calm-down corner. Regardless of how cluttered the rest of your house is, this is an area that really should have just a few items. Too much stuff will make it hard for your child to focus and choose what to do. You'll want to include items and toys that are known and comforting to your little one—not items to challenge her to try new or different activities. No need to spend much money; you likely already have or can make anything you want to include.
- No screens, tablets, or electronic toys in the calm-down corner, with the exception of an MP3 or CD player loaded with guided meditations. I'm not saying your child should never watch a TV show again. I'm just saying it shouldn't be here.
- This is not a time-out spot, and your child shouldn't be forced into it. It may be a spot she chooses instead of time-outs if you use time-outs in your house, but it should always be a place she goes willingly. You want your child to have positive associations with the calm-down corner, which won't be easy if it feels like a jail cell to her.

The calm-down corner is a sacred space where shouting, nagging, arguing, discussing, questioning, and negotiating are not allowed. This space isn't for figuring things out or rehashing problems; it's just for being, breathing, and doing quiet, soothing activities. That's all. Once you're there, you're safe.

What to Put in a Calm-Down Corner

Here are some toys and items that you and your child may want to consider putting in her calm-down corner. You may want to pay attention to what your child continues to show interest in, and if it seems useful to rotate out some items, go right ahead. But remember, the calm-down corner isn't about stimulation—it's about calming down—so don't feel as though you need to put something new in every week. Note: If anything on this list is likely to make a mess or noise that will stress you out, don't use it.

Sensory Toys and Items

- Beanbag chair or stress balls
- Play-Doh or modeling clay
- Silly Putty
- Lotion
- Smooth stones, possibly with calming words like "Breathe" or "Peace" written on them
- Small Zen garden tray with sand and a small rake
- Soft blanket or pillow
- Favorite stuffed animals

Listening Toys and Items

- Rain stick
- MP3 or CD player loaded with soothing music or guided meditations (choose a player without a screen, if possible)
- Mindfulness bells or a singing bowl

Observing Toys and Items

- Kaleidoscope
- Glitter wand, snow globe, or glitter jar (which can be easily made with directions available online)
- Flashlight
- Small battery-powered votive candles
- Magnifying glass
- Wall art or small statues that your child likes
- Favorite picture books or storybooks (can be related to mindfulness or not)

Smelling Toys and Items

- Scented rice or bean pillows (can be microwaved or put in the freezer if your child prefers something warm or cold)
- Scented markers
- Scratch-and-sniff stickers
- Lotion with scent

Breathing Toys and Items

- Pinwheels
- Bubbles
- Breathing buddy (a small stuffed toy that your child can put on her belly and rock to sleep with her breathing)
- Hoberman sphere to use as a breathing aid; children can inhale as they expand the sphere and exhale as they close it (Cohen Harper 2013)
- Yoga reminders (can be books, posters, or cards with different yoga poses on them)

Feeling and Compassion Toys and Items

- Wall poster of faces expressing different feelings
- Books about different feelings and experiences
- Small photo album with photographs of beloved friends and family members
- Paper and markers for drawing about feelings
- Stuffed toys with different facial expressions (such as Kimochis) that help children identify their feelings
- Favorite stuffed animals

If you don't have space in your home for a calm-down corner (or even a calm-down chair), another option is to create a breathing box or a breathing bag for your child containing items that she finds soothing. Any of the smaller toys or items in the previous list will work.

Try This: Make a Breathing Box

Find a shoebox or a small box with a lid and fill it with toys or items that your child will find soothing. (Or, you could put together a breathing bag, perhaps a small zippered cloth bag, which could be useful for school or travel.) If your child is old enough, be sure to fill it together. Some possibilities for the breathing box are some smooth stones with soothing words on them, a small notebook and some pens or markers, a small glitter wand (these are available in key-chain size), or an MP3 player and headphones. Find a special place in your child's room or backpack to keep the box, where she can easily find it when needed.

This chapter has suggested some different ways to create more time and space for mindfulness in your life and home. You may feel a sudden need to cancel all of your kid's activities, throw out half your stuff, and rearrange your entire house. Please don't do that. Instead, take a few days to just notice. Pay attention to your schedule, to the days when your child seems to feel the most exhausted or when you feel the most harried and hurried. Do you have any flexibility on those days? Can you cancel one activity or say no to one meeting?

Similarly, take a few moments to look around your house. Are there countertops, corners, or storage bins filled with old papers, half-finished art projects, crumpled homework assignments, or broken pieces from board games? Are they impacting your family's ability to get grounded and stay focused? If so, they might be worth cleaning or clearing out. If not, don't worry about it.

Finally, does your child already have a space in the house where she can take a few moments to breathe and relax? If so, that's great. Perhaps you can work together to pick a couple of items from this chapter to add to this space.

The goal here isn't to have a perfectly balanced schedule and a perfectly clean house. The goal is to discern what's going to make a difference for your family: where you and your kid can tolerate a bit of chaos and when you really need to slow down, schedule some free time, and create some mindful space in your home. From there, you can start talking with your child about the changes you're making and why you're making them. That's the topic of the next chapter.

CHAPTER 5

Talking About Mindfulness with Kids

From time to time, my daughter will complain about some sort of vague physical pain; her tummy aches or her leg hurts or her ear is throbbing. Most of the time, there's not much I can do about whatever is going on except snuggle her and reassure her that it won't last forever. I'll say something like, "I know your tummy hurts now, and I'm sorry about that. Just remember that it will feel better soon. What can I do to help you until it does?" This response to my daughter has evolved quite a bit since I started practicing mindfulness. I used to focus on making the pain go away, and then I would get frustrated with myself and my little girl when that didn't happen. Now, I try to remember to acknowledge her feelings, offer my help, and remind both of us that nothing lasts forever, whether it's a wonderful moment or an excruciating one. That small shift in focus, from feeling as though we are mired in our current experience to remembering that it's just a blip on the radar, can help us enjoy the pleasant moments more fully and suffer a bit less with the difficult ones.

This is just one example of how you can use words to help your child develop a more mindful perspective. Many of the activities in this book are experiential, as mindfulness is something that must be practiced directly if we are to reap the benefits; we can't just talk about it. Having said that, it's also true that words matter. The way we talk about our experience has the potential to shape our awareness of it and thus our reality. This chapter will explore a range of ideas, metaphors, and other ways of using words to help direct your child's attention and infuse moments of mindfulness into his daily experience. To start with, the basic definition of mindfulness bears repeating: noticing what is happening right here and now, in a friendly and curious way, and then choosing what to do next. That definition contains four ideas that you can highlight with your child: noticing, the here and now, kindness, and choice. This chapter will go into each of these ideas as well as a couple of other important concepts.

Noticing

It can be easy to notice thoughts, feelings, and sensations that are new or interesting or weird or really big. However, short of a truly brilliant idea or a broken bone, our children may not notice what is going on in their minds and bodies until they've become so overloaded that they can no longer ignore it. When that happens, kids are likely to lash out, either verbally or physically, in ways that are often unhelpful and may even make the situation worse. In those situations, the best thing to do is to help our children calm down and then talk to them about what happened. Fortunately, we can teach our children to pay attention to what is happening in their bodies and minds so that they can talk about their experience or ask for help before it's too late. We can practice explicitly with them, perhaps by doing a breathing or listening meditation as described in chapter 6, and we can also talk with them about this idea during calm moments. Here are some ideas for how to help your child get better at noticing.

Talk About What You Notice

Talking about what you notice is a very basic practice, but it's not something many of us do on a regular basis. The idea here is to talk about your experience with your child. For example, when I'm getting frustrated, I often walk into the kitchen, put my hands on the countertop, and take a few deep breaths. If I don't talk to my children about what I'm feeling and doing, they're not going to learn anything except that Mommy sometimes walks into the other room and then comes back. However, if I say something about how I'm noticing my shoulders getting tense or my face getting hot, or that I'm feeling like I'm about to yell, and that those are warning signs that I need to stop what I'm doing and take a few deep breaths, my daughters may begin to understand the value in paying attention to our bodies so that we can make better choices.

Notice When They Notice

Sometimes kids actually do a great job of talking about how they're feeling, either emotionally or physically. It's not always easy to hear this from them, especially if it's been a long day, they're whining, or we're exhausted. So a common response is to try to fix whatever is happening or distract our kids from it. However, each time we can acknowledge not just what they noticed but also that they noticed it at all, we're helping our children take an important first step toward a mindful approach to their experience. It's important that you find the words and style that work for you, but you can always say something like, "I'm so glad you noticed that you were sad and that you chose to tell me about it. Do you want to talk about it more?"

Another way to talk about this is to notice when your child is having what noted meditation teacher Joseph Goldstein calls an "about to" moment. It's a useful way to help your child notice when he's about to lose his temper or mouth off and that he can make a different choice. If you see that he is getting tense, or loud, or flushed, it may be helpful to observe with him that he's in an "about to" moment and that he has a chance to make a more skillful choice. It's not always easy for our children to hear this, so if you can get into the habit of noticing your own "about to" moments out loud ("I feel my jaw tightening and my shoulders tensing. I think I might be about to yell, so I probably need to go into the other room and take a few deep breaths"), it may help your child be a bit more responsive to your suggestions. In all likelihood, he is probably doing this particular sort of noticing from time to time anyway; the key is to make those moments a little less random and a little more intentional. Helping him notice the clues his body is giving him when he's having an "about to" moment is a great place to start.

Help Them Describe What They Notice

Children vary widely in their ability to recognize an emotion or sensation and put words to it, but many kids, and especially younger ones, may have a hard time with it. This is why they end up throwing a tantrum or hitting a sibling when they're sad or frustrated or hungry or tired; they've got something going on in their little minds or bodies, but they're not quite sure what it is, how to express it, or what to do it about it. We can help our children get better at expressing themselves in more skillful and helpful ways. The first step, especially for younger children, is to put words to their experience. "You're feeling jealous because I'm feeding your baby sister and not paying as much attention to you, which is why you threw your food." When we do this in a mindful way, just noticing and describing without judging or getting angry, over time our children will start to be able to notice and identify their internal experience without having to immediately act on it. You can ask older kids to talk about their feelings or to draw their feelings, journal about them, or pick a song that seems to match them.

Play What You Notice

It's not always easy to describe feelings. They may seem overwhelming and confusing, or talking about big feelings can feel embarrassing, shameful, or just too hard to do, especially when they're unpleasant. In these situations, it may be helpful to use dolls or action figures as stand-ins and to make up a story or a situation that you think might be similar to what is going on for your child. If you tell a story about how Superman had his feelings hurt when Batman wouldn't play with him, your child will make the connection with what may have happened to him. In addition, reading stories that might resonate with your child's experience, ranging from very simple board books about emotions to more complicated chapter books, can provide a useful way to begin to talk about difficult topics. Finally, most kids love to hear stories about their parents' lives. Sharing a story about a time when we were hurt or confused or ashamed, and how we thought about it and how it felt in our bodies, can help our children understand their experience and talk about it.

Turn on Your Noticing Brain

When it comes to experiencing and managing big emotions, there are two parts to our brain: the feelings part (the limbic system in the back, at the base of our skull) and the noticing part (the prefrontal cortex, just behind our foreheads). The cool thing about the brain is that it can't use both parts at the same time. When your child is stuck in his feelings brain, see if you can get him to turn on his noticing brain. Depending on his age, you might ask him to see whether he can notice the color blue, or notice your nose, or whatever funny or benign thing that might be just enough to pull his attention out of his limbic system and into his prefrontal cortex. Once he's calmed down, you can either move on with your day or spend a little time talking about what happened, depending on his age and mood and the situation.

Preview and Review

This next practice is a great way to mindfully bookend any experience with your child, which I learned from mother and parent coach Danya Handelsman (pers. comm.). Before you do whatever it is you're going to do, from having a casual snack to going on a family outing, talk to your child about what is likely to happen, and then talk about the experience after it's over. It may seem as though talking about the future and the past is the very opposite of being in the present moment; the difference is that in this activity you're making an intentional choice to spend some time planning and remembering rather than randomly getting swept up in the musings of your mind.

The goal behind previewing an event is to get our children ready to pay attention and to help them notice and let go of any worries, fears, or unreasonable expectations they may have, so they can be as present as possible for whatever does actually happen. Each time we remember what happened, we're teaching our children the value of intentionally taking some time to look back on the choices they've already made and to consider the results. In addition, reviewing can help children see the difference between their hopes and fears and what actually happened, so they can begin to understand the ways in which their thoughts can impact their reality in helpful or unhelpful ways.

Take a Mental Picture

Most children these days are used to having their picture taken, and many of them are getting behind the camera as well. It can be tempting to hand our children a smartphone or camera and encourage them to capture the moment, but using a camera or phone can very quickly and easily distract even the most mindful of us from the experience of the present moment. Another idea is to encourage your child to take a mental picture of whatever is happening. What is he noticing? What does he want to focus on? What does he want to include in the picture? What does he want to leave out?

What Will You Remember?

Asking your child what he will remember is similar to asking him to take a mental picture, but it can be helpful to have a variety of ways to talk about any given idea, so you can find one that resonates with your child. To use this strategy, at any given moment, you can ask your child what he will remember from this experience. Bear in mind that you're not looking for any specific answer, and it doesn't have to be something positive or happy. There is great value in noticing and being able to tolerate the more challenging or unpleasant moments in life. Ask your child what he will remember from the day, and be open to whatever he comes up with.

Exercise Your Mindful Muscle

Many kids love the idea of stretching and strengthening their bodies, and each time they practice mindfulness, they are strengthening the parts of their brain that help them stay calm, think clearly, and make good choices. You can remind your child that whenever he can take a moment to notice what is happening in his own thoughts, feelings, and bodily sensations and respond to that experience with kindness and acceptance, it's like his mind just did a workout at the gym.

Here and Now

In addition to helping your child notice his experience, you can also help him consciously direct his attention to the here and now. This practice will help him get grounded in the present moment and loosen his grip on the worries, fears, and regrets that can be so distracting and troubling. In addition, as your child gets better at being present, he will come to see situations with greater clarity and accuracy, which will help him pick the most skillful and effective response.

Some of the exercises already described can be useful in pointing your child's awareness back to the present moment. Here are a few more to try.

Three things about three things. If you notice that your little one is feeling distracted, overwhelmed, or bored, one way to get him into a different head space is to ask him to tell you three things about three things. He can choose any three things he wants—a sight, a sound, or even a thought that is passing through his mind. From there, ask him to tell you three things about whatever it is that he's noticing. Perhaps a small rubber ball caught his eye, and he can feel the texture and describe the color and talk about how it reminds him of his cousin who loves bouncy balls. Or maybe he noticed a pain in his toe, and he can let you know which toe it is, how far up his foot the pain goes, and whether it feels like a sharp prick or a dull ache. If he has a thought in his mind, he can tell you what the thought is, how that thought makes him feel, and what other thoughts are coming along behind those thoughts. Your child can choose something pleasant, something unpleasant, or something neutral, and it can be either interesting or not. If three things about three things is a bit too much, try three things about one thing, or any variation that works for you and your child.

The five senses. This is an activity you can lead your child through anytime he needs a little redirection back into the present moment. It's simple enough—ask him to describe something he is noticing with each of his five senses: sight, smell, hearing, taste, and touch. If your child has a hard time putting words to the taste in his mouth or the sound he's hearing, that's okay. All that matters is that he takes a moment to notice. While it may be tempting to pass judgment on your child's observations, to wish they were more pleasant or happy or interesting or insightful, or whatever, try to let go of those thoughts if they come, and just listen to and accept whatever he offers.

Feel your feet on the floor. Sometimes kids need a moment of physical contact with something firm or soft or fuzzy, whether it's a hard floor or a soft teddy bear, to get them back into the here and now. Kids also love alliteration, rhymes, and silly voices, so have your child put his hands on his head, his toe on a toy, or his nose on a rose. A few seconds of noticing a physical sensation can be enough to help your child find his grounding and get his focus.

You Are Not Your Thoughts

Remembering that we are not our thoughts is a powerful way to stay grounded in the present moment, and it's worth exploring more here. One of the greatest gifts of mindfulness practice, of learning to observe our thoughts, feelings, and bodily sensations without getting swept away by any of it, is that we come to see that our thoughts are not our reality, and they can dictate our experience only to the extent that we allow them to do so. Each time we can remind our children that they can choose their response to the ideas running through their minds, we are empowering them to make a choice about what they want to do with that particular blip on the radar. Is it worth taking seriously, or is it better left to beep its way right off the screen? Here are a few ideas for how you can use your words to help your child get a little distance from that chattering monkey in his mind.

Watch the traffic go by. This idea that we are not our thoughts is pretty abstract, so metaphors can be a great way to convey it. For example, comparing our thoughts to cars, which we can either hop into for a little trip around town or pass up entirely, is a great way to talk about this. If your little one is into dancing, you can talk about which ideas are worth a spin around the dance floor and which ones aren't going to make the cut. Maybe the thoughts are a parade going by that he can watch, or they are a conveyor belt or a roller coaster that he can get on or not. The goal is to pick a metaphor that acknowledges the constant motion of our thoughts; they're going to keep on coming whether we like it or not. You don't want your kid to get the idea that he should be able to stop his thoughts, but you want to find a way to help him remember that he can choose whether or not to jump into the fray.

Who's thinking that thought? This practice is a great way to help your child depersonalize whatever is going on in his head and not get caught up in the shame, blame, embarrassment, or intense frustration that can so often hitch a ride on the backs of unhelpful thoughts. It can be as easy as asking, "Who's thinking that thought? Tired Ryan? Hungry Ryan? Naggy Ryan?" If your child is having a hard time putting words to the part of him that seems to be at the controls of his brain, you can start by modeling this for him at various times in your day. I've been known to talk about how loud Grumpy Mommy is being today and how I need to find a way to help her calm down. Again, the details aren't important, but the goal is to find a way to describe the thinker as either a part of you or outside of you—that is, not all of you.

Name that monkey. Or that gremlin. Or that angry octopus. Once again, the idea is to help your child get a little head space, and attributing his thoughts to a crazy little monkey—or any real or imaginary animal or creature—can be a funny and effective way to do it. As you both get to know the monkey a little better, you'll get better at predicting when it's going to start spouting off some rather unhelpful ideas, and you'll also get better at figuring out what it needs to calm down.

This Too Shall Pass

Everything changes. This is a fundamental reality of our existence that we can all too easily lose sight of. When something is great, we want it to last forever, and when our experience is unpleasant or uninteresting, we can feel mired in it even as we are desperate for it to end. Remembering that it will pass, whatever it is, can lessen your child's suffering in difficult moments and increase his ability to appreciate wonderful experiences. Sometimes it can be as easy as reminding him that nothing lasts forever, but other times you may need different ways to communicate this reality. Here are a few ideas.

Life is like the weather. Even young children know that the weather changes; they can remember that it was rainy yesterday and sunny today or that it might snow tomorrow. This is a particularly great analogy not only because it's so easy to notice and remember weather changes but also because we can't control the weather, but we can decide whether we want to run around in the rain or hang out inside. Either way, and regardless of how we feel about it, if we wait it out, something different will come along.

Change is part of the deal. One of the mothers I interviewed shared this simple, straightforward, and totally accurate phrase with me, and I love it. Change is part of the deal, whatever the deal may be, and sometimes our kids just need to be reminded of that.

Riding the wave. If you have a beach-loving kid, it can be helpful to talk about the ocean, the waves, and the changing tides. A wave can seem huge as it's swelling up in front of you or even crashing over you, but within a few seconds, it's nothing more than bubbling foam creeping up on the sand. Similarly, our thoughts, feelings, and bodily sensations can feel completely overwhelming, as if we're going to drown in them. By talking to our children about riding those waves or waiting them out, we can help them remember that whatever they're experiencing will soon lessen in strength, like the tide going out or a wave that's run its course.

Kindness and Compassion

A kind, compassionate, and curious approach to our experience is key to mindfulness. It doesn't matter how much our kids learn to pay attention if they immediately judge or despise whatever it is they've just noticed. Each time they do that, they've immediately yanked themselves out of their mindful moment and handed the reins over to that little gremlin who can be so decidedly unhelpful. The thing is, it's not always easy to be nice to ourselves and those around us, especially in challenging or stressful moments. Like every other aspect of mindfulness, it's something we need to practice. I've included many more activities on this topic in chapter 6, but here are a few ways to model compassion and talk about it with your child.

What would a friend say? Asking your child what his friend would say or think about this is a great question when he can't seem to shake himself out of a negative head space. If he can't come up with some friendly self-talk, maybe he can remember what a good friend might say to him. Alternately, you could ask what he might say to a friend who is struggling.

Family appreciations. A simple but powerful practice, at dinner or other regular family gatherings, is to take a moment to go around the table and have each person share a brief appreciation about everyone else. This is not only a great way for all of you to feel more connected and valued but also an effective way to practice giving and receiving kindness. Finally, if your child knows that he will need to say something nice about everyone at the end of the day, he'll be more likely to start noticing small moments of kindness so that he'll have something to contribute.

Filling buckets. My husband came up with this practice based on the book *Have You Filled a Bucket Today?* by Carol McCloud (2006). You all sit in a circle, and when it's your turn, you hold your hands or arms in the shape of a bucket, and every other member of the family fills your bucket by sharing something they like or appreciate about you. Then you fill your own bucket by saying something nice about yourself.

Ambulance loving-kindness. My friend Sheila McCraith, who is the author of *Yell Less, Love More*, described sending friendly wishes to ambulances whenever they go racing past her car or home (pers. comm.). I love this idea for two reasons. First, it's another way to model responding to a seemingly irrelevant situation with kindness. Second, it reinforces the idea that there is value in being kind to people we don't even know and will likely never meet. It's all about helping our children strengthen their kindness muscle, so it will be strong enough when they really need it to do some heavy lifting in a challenging moment. A variation of this activity is animal loving-kindness; any animal that crosses our path, from a pet dog to a squirrel running up a tree to the bug we're so eager to shoo out the door, represents an opportunity to practice compassion.

Love yous. I learned about this practice from Jennifer Cohen Harper (pers. comm.), who is the author of *Little Flower Yoga*. This is a great activity to do at bedtime or whenever your child needs to feel safe and loved. It's quite simple: list all the people who love your little one. If you get a nice rhythm going, it can be almost like a mantra: "Mama loves you. Daddy loves you. Sister loves you…" The list can go on and on.

Choosing to Be Mindful

One of the most powerful and empowering aspects of mindfulness is that it is available to us at any moment; we just need to choose to come back to whatever is actually happening right now and get interested in it. There is no blame or shame for letting our minds wander. There is only the choice to become aware, over and over again. Here are a few ways to talk to your child about how to do this.

You can always start over. Sometimes we need to remind our children of this fundamental truth in really basic language: you can always start over. Always.

Request a reboot. Kids who spend any time at all on computers will love this one. They know that when the computer keeps freezing up or not responding, you need to shut it down for a minute before rebooting it. You can let your child know that no matter what's happening, he can request a reboot. Any time. If you feel like there needs to be some discussion about whatever happened, that's okay, but let your kid have his reboot and enough time to get into a better place before you start talking about it. The conversation will likely go better anyway.

Clean the whiteboard. This is similar to requesting a reboot. Again, it's all about finding the words that resonate with your child. If your kid is familiar with chalkboards or whiteboards, you can remind him that what's on the board doesn't matter. You can always erase it and write a new message or draw a different picture.

Magic moment. I learned this phrase from noted meditation teacher Sharon Salzberg (2010). Any moment when we notice what is happening is a magic moment because it's when we have a real opportunity to make a different choice. Talking about this with your child and noticing out loud when you are having a magic moment can help him begin to identify these moments for himself.

There are many ways to talk about mindfulness with our children. Hopefully, this chapter has given you some ideas to get started. What's most important is to find the language and metaphors that resonate with you and your child. If you stick to the basic concepts—noticing the present moment with kindness and compassion so we can choose our behavior—you can't go wrong.

CHAPTER 6

Your Mindfulness Toy Box

By now you should have a good sense of what mindfulness is, how and why it works, and how to introduce it to your child. This chapter will explore a number of ways to deepen and expand your practice of mindfulness with your child. The first half offers some breathing exercises and other activities that can help children manage some of the most challenging times of the day: mornings, evenings, meals, and transitions, such as getting ready for school or leaving a play date. The second half of the chapter teaches a range of skills that can help your child reduce her stress, get a handle on big emotions, and strengthen her ability to pay attention, among other things. As I've said before, the more you are practicing mindfulness on your own and with your child, the more likely your child will be interested in trying out new ways of paying attention, noticing her experience, and responding to herself and others with kindness and compassion.

As you try out the different exercises, you'll want to concentrate on what works for your child. If there's something that piques your interest, but you're not sure your child will be into it, or if you try it and it really doesn't work, that's okay. Remember, however, that nothing lasts forever and children will change.

Maybe an exercise is not the right match for your child, or maybe it's not the right match for her right now.

Some of these practices might seem similar to each other, and in some ways they are. Again, I've offered a variety of wordings and ways to think about each idea, so you can find one that works for your family. Sometimes it just takes a different word or a small shift in the way we do something to make it work. There is no one perfect way to practice mindfulness, but there are an infinite number of ways to do it well. They all come back to paying attention with kindness and curiosity, however that may look for each of us. Remember that you know your child best, and you can always begin again, no matter how long it's been since you've taken a deep breath together or stopped to notice what is actually happening.

Another word of advice: don't push if you notice resistance. This may come in the form of outright refusal to participate, excessive silliness, or frequent subject changes. When that happens, let it go. Getting into a power struggle over a mindfulness exercise will probably stress you out and make your child less likely to be interested in trying again later. Similarly, acknowledging effort is better than acknowledging outcome. For example, if your child wants to try a sitting meditation but gets fidgety after ten or twenty seconds, that's okay. Let her know that you're proud of her for trying and that you'd love to try again when she's ready.

Don't forget to practice in the calm moments. That's the ideal time for everyone in the family to learn how to use these activities to get focused and grounded, and the more you've all practiced, the more successful you'll be in the difficult moments.

Finally, please remember that any activity can be a mindful moment or not, depending on how you approach it with your child. There is no right or wrong way to do any of the practices described here, so you don't need to worry about rules or outcomes. As long as you're staying present, open, and accepting to whatever comes up, you're doing it right.

Breathing

Breathing is a core mindfulness practice and a skillful way to approach virtually any challenging moment. Taking a few mindful breaths can help children use their words, move out of tantrums more quickly, deal with boredom, and make a conscious choice not to lash out when they're frustrated. Here are a few ways to teach your child to breathe intentionally.

Hand-on-heart breathing. You can have your child place her hand on your heart, or you can place your hand on her heart, or you can each hold a hand to your own chest. Breathe. Feel yourself and each other breathing.

Back-to-back breathing. Sit down with your back up against your child's back. Breathe together. Variation: Lie next to each other and each notice your breathing. If your child is not interested in this practice, just focus on your own breathing. You will get and stay calm more quickly, and your little one won't be far behind.

Count your breaths. It's not easy to keep track of one's breathing, even for grown-ups! Counting each breath, up to five or ten before starting again, is a great way to stay as focused as possible. If you lose count, you can go back to one and start again.

Count the beads on a breathing bracelet. Many religious traditions use beaded bracelets or necklaces to help practitioners stay focused on their prayers. A small beaded *breathing bracelet* can help your child count her breaths while also giving her something to do with her hands. You can order bracelets online or, even better, head to the local craft store and make them together.

Finger-counting breathing. Hold your hand up and spread your fingers out wide. Trace your fingers as you breathe. Breathe in as you trace up each finger and breathe out as you trace back down.

Blow bubbles. Many children, especially younger ones, have a hard time figuring out how to pay attention to their breathing. Blowing bubbles, dandelions, or pinwheels can be a great way to help them figure out how to breathe in and out intentionally.

Blow out the candles. Hold up your fingers and pretend they are birthday candles. Blow out the candles one at a time, taking a nice long inhale between each one.

Rock your teddy to sleep. Have your child choose a small stuffed animal or toy that will fit on her belly and then have her rock it to sleep by breathing in and out slowly.

Smell the flowers, blow the bubbles. This is a great way to practice nose and mouth breathing. Have your child pretend to hold a flower in one hand and a bubble blower in the other one. As she brings the "flower" up to her nose, she breathes in the scent, and then as she brings the "bubble wand" up to her mouth, she blows out the bubbles. The goal is to get her breathing in a steady rhythm, supported by the motion of her hands.

Remember, you can always come back to breathing. This is a fundamental practice of mindfulness, because your breath will always be there, no matter what else is going on. Your child doesn't have to remember how to sit or what to say or anything else. So, when you're freaking out or your child is spinning out of control, and neither of you seems to know how to get a handle on things, just come back to breathing.

Different Situations

Incorporating mindfulness exercises into your daily routines, transition times, or predictably chaotic moments of the day can help your child learn to cope with challenging situations and develop skillful habits that will serve her well throughout her life.

Mornings

As many parents know, getting through the morning routine can be, well, challenging. There's often a lot to get done in a short amount of time, and sleepy kids may have a hard time getting motivated. Besides working with your child to get as much done as you can the night before, such as making lunches, packing backpacks, and picking out clothes, here are a few other steps that may make for a more mindful morning.

Find five more minutes. If your family is feeling perpetually rushed in the mornings, see if you can find five more minutes somewhere in your schedule. Whether it's doing even more prep the night before or waking up a bit earlier, that five minutes can make a difference, especially if you use the time to get into a more mindful head space.

Connect. Many children benefit from a few moments of reconnecting with their parents in the morning. It may seem like you don't have time, but even a brief mindful snuggle or chat may help the rest of the morning go more smoothly.

Prayers and mantras. Many religious traditions and faiths have a tradition of morning prayers. Expressing gratitude for the new morning and setting an intention for the day, such as kindness, acceptance, patience, or gratitude, can help everyone get into a positive head space. Mantras, which are described in greater depth later in this chapter, can also be useful in the morning to help everyone get grounded and focused.

Notice the weather. Connecting to the natural world is a quick and effective way to come back to the present moment so you can move forward in thoughtful and intentional ways. Taking a moment to look out the window or step outside can help everyone get ready for the day.

Check the calendar. Checking the calendar and noticing the day and date is a useful way to help kids become aware of the passage of time and the rhythm of the week. It can also help them know what to expect each day, which decreases anxiety and helps children feel more empowered.

Plan for the day. In addition to checking the calendar, you can take a moment to talk your child through the plan for the entire day: get ready for school, go to school, soccer practice after school, homework, dinner, bath, bedtime. Whatever we can do to help children know what is coming next can help them move more smoothly through transitions.

Bedtime

Many children have a hard time settling their mind and body at bedtime. Fortunately, there are several ways to help your child successfully transition to sleep. In addition to the practices suggested in this section, you may want to consider turning off screens an hour before bedtime, dimming lights, choosing quiet activities, and maintaining a consistent bedtime with a predictable routine whenever possible.

Remember the day. This is a great way to settle a busy mind. Have your child remember what she did that day, starting from when she woke up to the present moment. The goal is to get into a steady rhythm of describing the day's events without getting stuck in commentary or revisions. It might look something like this: "I woke up, I went to the bathroom, I brushed my teeth and combed my hair, I got dressed, I went downstairs and ate a waffle, I played with my Batman car, I put on my shoes and coat…" Whenever our children do this, they are both practicing sustaining their attention and learning to observe the activities of their day and their mind without getting too caught up in them, which is a fundamental mindfulness skill. This can be done out loud or silently; if you can teach your child to do it in her head, she may fall asleep before she even gets to lunchtime.

Guided meditations and visualizations. There are a number of guided meditations and visualizations that can help your child relax at the end of the day. Helping your child choose a happy place, real or imagined, or remember a great vacation is a great place to start, or you can tell a story in which your child is the main character. Keep in mind that these stories aren't about slaying dragons; they're about helping your child imagine herself in a calm, happy place, whatever that looks like for her, and then helping her stay there. If you have a hard time making them up yourself, there are a number of excellent books and CDs available (see resources).

Just relax. We know from the research and common sense that instructing someone to go to sleep is rarely effective. The harder we try to force ourselves to sleep, the more anxious we are likely to become. So don't tell your child to go to sleep. Instead, tell her she doesn't have to sleep, but she does need to relax quietly, and she might want to think about something that makes her happy, maybe something fun that happened at school or a movie she really enjoyed. The sleep will come.

Loving-kindness at bedtime. Sending love and kind wishes to ourselves and others is a foundational meditation practice (see chapter 2) and an effective way to help your child focus, channel her excess energy in a positive way, and feel very loved and taken care of. You can do this informally by talking about the people in your life whom you love and who love you and by sending happy thoughts to all of them, or you can do it more formally by repeating specific phrases. This will be most effective if you and your child decide on the wording together. This is my favorite version: *May I be happy, May I be healthy, May I be safe, May I feel loved.* After your child has directed the happy thoughts to herself, she can send them to people in her family, friends, people she interacts with regularly but doesn't know very well (the crossing guard, the librarian), and then the whole world. A variation is the practice of "love yous" described in chapter 5.

The little box of worries. Have your child decorate a small box with a lid, so she will have a place to put her worries at night. You can keep a bowl of small stones or marbles to represent each worry, or use slips of paper to jot them down. Putting them in the box is a very concrete way to help your little one let go of her worries. You can remind her that they will still be there in the morning if she's not done thinking about them. If she can't remember her worries when she wakes up, it may mean that she's done worrying about that issue, at least for now.

Put the worry dolls to sleep. You can buy or make small worry dolls, and then at night your child can whisper a worry to each doll. Your little one can then put the dolls, along with her worries, to sleep, either under her pillow or in a small box, perhaps with a tiny tissue for a blanket.

Counting down. This is something my husband started doing when our older daughter was an infant, and several of the parents I interviewed talked about doing the same thing. Pick a number—ten or twenty is a good place to start—and then count down from there. You can start with a slightly louder voice and then get quieter with each number, or you can calmly sing the numbers as you count. It's a great way to help children focus on your voice and the counting, and knowing what's coming next is always relaxing.

Meals

When we slow down and pay attention to what we're eating, rather than shoveling bite after bite into our mouths while our eyes are glued to the TV or our smartphones, we enjoy our food more and make healthier eating choices. Here are some ideas for how to share this practice with your whole family.

Two-minute meditation or silence before meals. You can use a timer on your smartphone or the clock on the wall. Take a moment or two to sit silently before the meal, focusing on your breathing. You can encourage your child to do the same, but don't nag her about it or worry about whether she's actually meditating or not. As long as she's being relatively quiet and calm, call it a win.

Blessings before meals. You can draw on your religious or cultural tradition, or you can work with your family to come up with a few words that help you all feel calm, centered, and grateful for the food you are about to enjoy. You can recite the blessing together or take turns.

Eat when you're eating. Just eat. Make a rule in your home that for at least one meal each day, there are no books, screens, toys, or crafts on the table. Being able to eat without distraction is a great way to learn to pay attention to a potentially boring activity, and it's a skill that will serve your child well throughout her life.

Play with your food. Don't get me wrong. I'm a big fan of table manners, and I'm constantly telling my girls not to play with their food. But sometimes taking the time to explore what's on the plate can make dinnertime more fun and interesting, and it's a great way to practice mindfulness. Ask your little one some questions about her food. What color is it? What does it smell like? Taste like? How does it feel? You can make this fun by asking your child to savor the flavor or to notice what the nose knows.

Put the fork down between bites. This is a great way to help your child eat a little more slowly and pay attention to what she's doing and what she's eating. Bite. Fork down. Bite. Fork down. Repeat.

Check in with your body before you clean your plate or fill it again. This is a simple yet powerful practice that can help your child learn to pay attention to her appetite and her tummy and to respond appropriately. When she declares herself to be done or asks for more, encourage her to check in with her body first.

The chewing game. Can you chew each bite ten times? Twenty times? Again, it's about slowing down and paying attention, but if you can make chewing your food into a game or a fun competition, your kid might be more likely to give it a shot.

Transitions and Chaotic Moments

Moving the family from one activity to the next can be a source of stress, whether it involves rushing to get out the door to school, leaving a birthday party, or heading upstairs to bed. These transitions can be as stressful for parents as they are for children. Anything you can do to stay calm will help your kid stay focused on what she needs to do next.

Remember Your ABCs. I love this practice from *A Still Quiet Place*, by Amy Saltzman (2014). A is for Attention. When things get busy or chaotic or we don't know what to do, we can always stop what we are doing and pay attention. B is for Breath. Paying attention to our breath can help us get grounded and calm, so we can make a better choice. C is for Choose. Breathing mindfully can help us make a more skillful choice about what to do next.

Preview the transition. You may have a good sense of what's coming next, such as what needs to get done before you can leave the house or how long you will need to wait before the doctor calls you in. Your child may not have that information. Describing each step and what to expect can help ease anxiety and frustration.

What will you remember? This practice (described in greater detail in chapter 5) is particularly useful when your child is having a hard time with endings or leave-takings. Taking the time to remember the event and discuss it lets her know that you're taking her experience seriously, and it will help solidify the memory in her mind.

Finger hugs. Kids often crave or benefit from our attention precisely when we feel too busy to give it. Taking a brief moment to intertwine fingers can be enough to bring your child's attention back to the present moment and help her feel more connected and grounded.

Three magic breaths. This exercise, which was introduced in chapter 2, is worth bringing up again. Kids love anything to do with magic, and the power of taking just a few intentional breaths is nothing short of magical. At any point in the day, when you want to get calm and focused so you can make skillful choices about what to do next, you and your child can take three magic breaths together.

Skills

There are a wide range of practices and activities that can strengthen your child's ability to pay attention, act with kindness, and manage big feelings and difficult situations as skillfully as possible.

Noticing the Present Moment

Paying attention to the present moment is an effective way to get a little distance from the endless stream of thoughts and feelings that can feel so overwhelming at times. This doesn't always come naturally, but the more we do it, the better we get at it. Here are a few activities that will help your kid practice coming back to the here and now.

Watching bubbles. There's something about watching bubbles float away that seems to have a calming effect on children and adults alike. This is also a lovely way to remind children that nothing lasts forever, but that doesn't mean we can't enjoy the bubbles while they're around.

Watching the glitter fall. Shaking up a snow globe or glitter wand is a concrete and effective way for children to calm their agitated minds and bodies. The swirling glitter is like their unsettled thoughts and feelings, and as children focus on the falling glitter, their minds settle. The picture book *Moody Cow Meditates* (MacLean 2009) incorporates this practice into a sweet story about a little cow having a very bad day.

Noticing walks. Some parents call these "walks to nowhere." These walks (see chapter 1) aren't about exercise, and they're not about getting anywhere. They're about walking and noticing what comes up along the way. These can also be a great opportunity to do a little preview and review with your child if she needs a little more direction or inspiration for the walk (see chapter 5).

The sky game. This simple practice was suggested by one of the parents I interviewed while writing this book. When her kids get grumpy or antsy or they start bickering, she'll tell them to look at the sky. This requires them to stop whatever they are doing, and if they're indoors, it means they have to go to a window, so they can see the sky. Sometimes there's a bird or a cool cloud to notice, and sometimes the mere act of getting a little perspective can help kids get into a better head space. This is a great activity to do in the car or for kids who are having a hard time being interested in a family hike or walk.

Draw what you see. There's no better way to pay close attention to what's around us than by having to recreate it. Asking children to draw something they see is a fun and effective way to get them to focus and sustain their attention. They can pick what they want to draw, or you can create some fun still lifes with toys, food, or random household objects. Remember, it's not about how well your child draws, so please don't comment on the quality of the picture.

Paying Attention

There are so many great ways to help our children practice paying attention, and many of them are games. I've listed a few here, but any activity that helps your child to slow down, pay attention, or use her body carefully is a great place to start!

Memory. This card-matching game requires kids to pay attention to remember where the cards that match are. There are many versions, and you can even make one at home. A deck of cards is made up of pairs of matching pictures. Lay out all the cards, with picture sides facing down on a table or on the floor, and then players alternate turning over two cards at a time. If the cards match, the player gets to keep them and gets another turn. If the cards don't match, the player turns the cards back over again, and another player tries to find a matching pair. The goal is to collect the most matching pairs. With younger children, you may want to start with as few as six cards, but eventually you can lay out twenty or more cards.

The "what's different?" game. This is an easy and fun game you can put together quickly at home. Place several household objects, such as a pen, a button, a spoon, a small stuffed animal, stickers, a bracelet, and a race car, on a cookie tray. Set a timer for thirty seconds or so, and have your child observe the items during that time. Have her look away while you remove one or two things, then see if she can tell you which ones are missing. This game is also fun to play with more than one child.

Jenga. This classic game involves building a tower of wooden blocks and then pulling the blocks out one at a time without toppling the tower. Jenga helps build concentration and body awareness.

Twister. Twister is all about body awareness and stretching. Your kid won't even realize she's developing useful skills as she puts right hand on red.

Chess or checkers. These games require your child to slow down, pay attention, consider the other player's perspective, and make choices, which are all great mindfulness skills.

Puzzles. Puzzles require children to hold sustained attention, notice carefully, and use their imagination to consider how the different pieces might fit together.

Building-block or Lego towers. It can be so easy to forget that play is how kids learn to slow down, notice, and make choices, even if it's just which Lego to use.

Knitting, coloring, and other crafts. Any activity that helps your child access her creative side is always a bonus. The repetitive nature of knitting, coloring, sewing, and similar crafts can be quite mindful.

Photography. Photography is a great metaphor for mindfulness, because it's all about noticing what's going on around you and choosing what to focus on. Thanks to the wonders of digital photography and the availability of inexpensive cameras, not to mention how much kids love screens, this is a great activity that many children enjoy.

Reading books. Among many benefits, reading out loud to your child is a sneaky and fun way to give her a chance to practice paying attention and listening well. In addition, reading books specifically about mindfulness-related concepts will help introduce these ideas to your child in new and interesting ways, and it will give both of you a shared language to come back to at another time. I've listed several of these books in the resources section.

Connection and Compassion

It can feel so hard to find our way into a place of compassion or kindness precisely when we all need it the most. The more we can create opportunities for our children to be intentionally kind, thoughtful, and grateful in their daily lives, the better they will get at it. Here are a few suggestions.

Happy wishes. In order to get better at anything, we have to practice doing it. A great way to help our kids get into the habit of being nice is to practice it. Literally. With metta (the loving-kindness practice introduced in chapter 2), you can direct kind wishes toward yourself, friends and family, people you don't know well, people who challenge you, and the entire world. The point of sending these happy wishes is not to get the other person to be happier, necessarily, but to train your mind for kindness. You can repeat these phrases during silent meditation, or you can write them down or repeat them out loud. I like to use the phrases "May you be happy. May you be healthy. May you be safe. May you feel loved." If those words don't sound right to you, you can change them however you want. Options include "I wish you happiness" or "I hope you are healthy." There are a couple of ways to introduce this practice to your child. You can say the phrases out loud at bedtime, or you can invite your child to meditate with you and teach her how to do it.

Stealth compassion. I got this idea from Chris Willard (2010), and I think it's great. Kids love being sneaky, and this is a lovely way for them to do it. The cool thing about mindfulness is that no one needs to know you're practicing it. Children can send secret happy wishes to their friends, teachers, kids who are bothering them, and, yes, even their parents. It's like they're building an invisible force field of kindness around themselves that no one can penetrate, no matter what.

Mindful body writing. This is a sweet way to connect with children while also helping them pay attention to their bodily sensations. Use your fingers to trace designs or words on your kid's back and have her try to guess what you're drawing.

Hug it out. This is like a regular hug or snuggle but with the added bonus of paying attention. Our kids won't let us snuggle them forever, so enjoy it while you can. In addition, your child will learn what it feels like to be truly connected physically with someone who is giving them their full attention.

Gratitude practice. The research on the benefits of gratitude is pretty amazing; it has been linked to increased resilience and happiness, stronger relationships, better sleep, and less stress. There are many ways to help children start a gratitude practice, and the best way to get them interested is to do it alongside them. You can go around the dinner table and each share one thing you're grateful for. Alternately, you can take turns writing in a gratitude journal, or you can leave notes in a gratitude jar that you can read later (see how to make an appreciation jar in chapter 4).

Highlights and lowlights. This is a great way for the entire family to express their appreciation for each other and to practice mindfully listening to, and accepting, each other's experiences, no matter what they may be. During family dinner, family meetings, or any time when you are all together, you can each share a highlight and a lowlight from your day. A variation of this is "Rose, Bud, and Thorn," in which everyone shares the best part of their day, the worst, and what's coming up next for them. Alternately, you can all share your news of the day, whatever it may be.

Be where they are. This is a fundamental compassion practice, and the best way we can teach it to our children is by modeling it for and with them. It sounds easy, but it's not, especially when our kids are being unpleasant or annoying, or making choices that we disagree with. However, when we can connect with their experience (as well as our own), they will feel less stuck, less alone, and more likely to get back on the right track sooner. A great way to intentionally get better at this is by doing it when it's easier. Take five or ten minutes at a time when your kid is in a good space to put your phone away, turn off the TV, and go with whatever she wants to do. Make a point of listening to her and following her lead. The more you can do this when things are calm, the easier it will be to do when the situation gets tense.

Body Awareness and Relaxation

Many children struggle with body awareness, physical tension, or restlessness. Here are some tips to help your little one start to notice her body and calm it down.

Quick body check-in. Sometimes the mere act of asking our children to check in with their bodies is enough.

Body scan/progressive muscle relaxation. This is a longer version of the CALM practice described in chapter 1. In this guided meditation, you ask your child to direct her attention to each part of her body, from her toes to the top of her head or vice versa. You can encourage your child either to relax the muscles in her body as she notices them or to just notice them and move on. There are many free audio versions and scripts available online; search "body scan for kids" or "progressive muscle relaxation for kids."

Cooked spaghetti and tin man. This is a much shorter and sillier way to teach children to intentionally relax their bodies. When you yell out "tin man!" your child has to straighten up and tense up, and then when you call out "cooked spaghetti!" she goes all limp. A variation of this is the spaghetti test: your child has to go from raw spaghetti to cooked spaghetti, relaxing more and more along the way.

Starfish stretch. I love this practice from Susan Kaiser Greenland (2010). First, describe a starfish: it has five arms that all meet in its center, and the starfish does everything from its center, including breathing. Then, to do the starfish stretch, have your child lie on the ground, and as she breathes into her center, she stretches her neck, arms, and legs as much as she can. As she breathes out, she relaxes and rests on the floor. Repeat as many times as you'd both like.

Dancing. If your child can't stop moving, then let her move. Turn on some tunes and get dancing. Wiggle out your sillies. Go outside and run around the yard or the block. Sometimes you gotta go with the flow.

Yoga. Yoga is an effective way for your child to move, stretch, and learn to focus her attention on her body. The resources section lists some great books and cards for practicing yoga with kids. Your local library may also be a good resource. One note: don't get too worried about whether your child does the pose right or holds it long enough, especially with a younger kid. The goal here is to introduce your kid to some new ways to move and experience her body and for her to have fun while she's doing it.

Find a class. As my wise grandmother—who raised seven children and helped raise numerous grandchildren—once told me, parents can't teach their children everything. An art, gymnastics, dance, martial arts, yoga, or a mindfulness-for-children class could be a great way for your child to learn some new ideas, activities, and skills that can supplement and support your home practice.

Calming Down

As I have mentioned before, there is no such thing as crisis meditation. We adults can't effectively start a new activity or practice when we're overwhelmed by big emotions, and it's no different for our children. However, there are a number of ways we can help our kids calm down when they're feeling angry, sad, frustrated, or overwhelmed, and several are listed below.

One important note: whatever you do to soothe your child will be most effective if you can start by connecting with her and understanding her experience. This may not be easy if you're feeling upset or annoyed by your child's behavior, and you may need to get yourself calm first, which will be easier if you've been practicing all along. In addition, you can practice any of the following ideas right alongside your child, which will help you both calm down together.

Breathing and body awareness practices are a great way to soothe big emotions, so if there are any such that your child prefers, those are a great place to start. Snow globes, glitter wands, and smooth stones may be useful in these moments. Here are some more ideas.

Mantras. A mantra is a word or a phrase that our children can repeat silently or out loud to help them focus their minds, calm their energy, and get them back on track. When choosing a mantra, there are a few things to keep in mind. First, mantras should be simple, straightforward, and easy to remember. Your child can have as many mantras as she'd like, and they may change with time, but the point is to choose something that will easily come to mind in difficult moments, so you don't want to switch too often. Second, mantras will be more effective if they come from your child, so follow her lead. Finally, it may help if the mantra is related to the details of the situation. For example,

"I am safe" or "I can do this" can help your child skillfully manage challenging physical moments, while "This too shall pass" can help her remember that a difficult situation won't last forever. Mantras can also be silly words, nonsensical sounds, brief prayers, or simple melodies, or they may be something that helps your child remember what to do in a difficult moment, such as "Breathe," "Go slowly," or "Be kind."

Take a line from TV. Lyrics or phrases from popular shows or movies are always fun for kids. "Hakuna Matata" from *The Lion King* reminded a generation of kids to take a break from their worries. This generation loves to "let it go," thanks to Disney's *Frozen*. *Mary Poppins* taught us to say "supercalifragilisticexpialidocious" when we don't know what else to say, and each episode of the PBS cartoon *Daniel Tiger's Neighborhood* is based on a short song with an important lesson, such as "When something seems bad, turn it around and find something good."

Count your way to calm. This is a variation on the mantra (and was already mentioned as a possible bedtime practice). Sometimes counting up or down from one to ten can distract your child just long enough for her to loosen her grip on whatever is going on. If your little one doesn't yet know her numbers to ten, she can count to three and then start again. Singing a favorite song can achieve the same effect.

Plug in to check in. There are great apps, CDs, and MP3s of guided meditations available online. A few are listed in the resources section. Letting your child take a few minutes to put on some headphones and spend some moments alone can be a great way for her to calm down.

Holding tight. Many children respond well to the physical pressure of a firm hug. If your child is having a hard time calming down, try a big, loving hug. Alternately, you can wrap your child in a blanket, not unlike a swaddle, and then hug your little baby burrito.

Love your lovey. Don't underestimate the power of a beloved toy. No matter what else is going on, a favorite blanket or stuffed animal can be a powerful cue to help your child calm down. If your child doesn't already have one, you may want to consider getting her something small and replaceable. A word of advice: never expect your child to share her lovey, regardless of what your other rules about sharing may be. The lovey is for soothing; it's not a carrot or a stick and shouldn't be used for bribery or punishment.

Soothing bath. A warm bath can be soothing to your little one. You can make a warm bath even more soothing by adding bubbles or some lavender scent. These baths aren't about scrubbing or getting clean; they're just about relaxing in the warm water. Be sure to wrap her up in a large soft towel afterward.

Listening

Who among us doesn't wish our kids were a little more consistent in their ability to listen? As mentioned, a great way to encourage good listening is by reading aloud to your child. There are also many benefits to practicing listening meditation. Noticing and paying attention to sounds can be easier than paying attention to our breathing. Here are a few more ideas to get you started.

Listening to music. It's always easiest to start a new practice with something simple and enjoyable. A few moments of listening to a favorite song can become extra special when you frame it as a meditation practice that you can do together. You can let your child know that the goal is not to listen hard but rather to notice when you've stopped listening to the music and started listening to your own thoughts and then go back to the song.

Three small sounds. This is a great way to help your child get used to being in silence. You can do this activity together during quiet moments, times when your child needs to calm down, or during transition times that aren't going as smoothly as you'd hope. Get quiet with your little one and ask her to tell you when she's heard three small sounds. That's it.

The silent game. This is a way to sneak in a few minutes of listening meditation, and it works particularly well in the car. Everyone stays silent until you get to the next stoplight or intersection, at which point you each describe three sounds that you heard.

Singing bowl. Singing bowls come in a variety of sizes, and you play them by striking the rim with a padded mallet. Allowing children to strike the bell can be a great way to get them interested, and from there the goal is to listen to the fading sound of the bell until they can't hear it anymore.

Draw what you hear. Put on some music. Ask your child to draw what she hears and then have her tell you all about it.

Insight and Self-Awareness

One of the amazing side effects of slowing down and paying attention to our thoughts, feelings, and sensations is that we start to get some insight and clarity into what triggers us, what hurts us, what soothes us, and what calms us down. Children vary greatly in their ability to know themselves, and every activity in this book will get them one step closer to understanding who they are, how they function, and what they need. Here are a few more practices that might help.

Journaling. Journals can be a great way for children to express themselves and get their feelings out by exploring them on paper. Many kids enjoy having a space to write or draw in that is just their own, to use how they want. (The journals with tiny padlocks can be extra fun for kids, but make sure to put the spare key someplace safe.) For your child to make the best use of her journal, it may be useful to remember two basic rules: first, the journal is a safe space where your kid can write or draw anything she wants. Anything. Second, you won't read or look at the journal unless you are invited to do so. If your child needs a little more guidance or structure in a particular moment, you can suggest that she make a gratitude list, describe the day, list three things she notices in that moment, or write a kind letter to herself.

Emotion tracking sheet. This is a straightforward way to help your child get a sense of how she's feeling. You can create a basic grid with days of the week across the top of the sheet and times of day down one side; you may want to pick some times that your child is likely to be home and will have a minute to check in with herself. You can buy stickers with different mood faces on them, or you can have your child draw or write her feelings at the moment. The goal here is not to report happy feelings all the time or even to increase the number of happy feelings. It's just about taking the time to notice and report whatever feeling she's having.

Personal weather report. This is a variation of the emotion tracking sheet, and it can be a great way for kids to get some insight into their own experiences. It also can help them get some distance from whatever is happening and remember that it's not going to last forever, no matter what it is. There are a variety of ways to help your child give a weather report; you can make it into a ritual that you do together each day, either in the morning or at the end of the school day. Alternately, you can create a board with some pictures of the weather that your child can Velcro into place, or you can ask her to check in with her report when you're not sure what else is going on or how she's doing. Is her internal weather sunny and calm? Rainy? Stormy? How does it feel?

Stoplight check-in. If you're not sure how your child is doing, and it doesn't seem like a great time to get into a big conversation about feelings, you can ask her for a quick stoplight check-in. Green means everything is going well; your child is ready to get on with the day. Yellow means things are a bit iffy, and she might need to move a little more slowly or get a little extra support until everything calms down. Red means there's a problem, and it's time to stop, connect, and figure out what she needs in that moment. A yellow or red stoplight will likely require some kind of follow-up conversation (at least initially), but over time you may develop a plan with your child so you both know what to do if the light isn't green.

Creating Space

Children can easily get stuck in unhelpful ruts, throwing tantrums, taking a negative view of things, or letting their thoughts run away with them. It can be tempting to try to solve the problem at hand, perhaps by talking or reasoning them into a better head space, but that's not always effective. Sometimes the best course of action is to do something drastically different, something that will basically yank your kid out of whatever alternate universe she's in and back into reality. Here are a couple of ideas for how to do that.

Disconnect to reconnect. Technology can be useful, but it's important to notice when it's not so helpful. Sometimes our kids need to step away from the computer and the homework that is making them crazy; sometimes they need to put down the smartphone or tablet that has kept them on the couch too long when they really need to eat, move, or sleep. Depending on the situation, your child may need a few minutes of stretching or dancing before getting back to her homework, or she may need to unplug for several hours or days. There may be a fair amount of resistance to this last intervention, but stick with it. It's worth it. This will go more smoothly if you also put away your computer and phone, and you'll probably feel better too.

Spend some time in the calm-down corner. If you or your child has forgotten about the calm-down corner, this may be a good time to revisit it.

Turn off the day. We all have those days that just feel like a wash. The ability to notice and accept those days, and to remember that tomorrow is a new day, can free us from fighting against them in unproductive ways. Turning off the day may mean letting a stressed or sick kid stay home from school, agreeing to turn in an assignment late or to miss an athletic practice, or just going to bed a little earlier than usual. We all have bad days, and the better we get at just accepting them, the more skillfully we'll be able to respond to them.

Get outside to go inside. Again, there's something about being outside that helps most kids get out of their own minds, move their bodies, calm down, have fun, and get a little clarity about whatever is going on (see chapter 4). Some kids may think of this as just playtime outside, and that's fine. Their play is their work, so let them get to it. Other children may find the outdoors a good place to practice some breathing, listening, or walking meditations. They may have an easier time of it when they're not distracted by screens, toys, homework, or whatever else is waiting for them back in the house. One note: we usually think of outside time happening during the day, but taking our kids out at night so they can notice the night sky and the stars, can also be a powerful way to shift their perspective.

Hopefully, these practices and the ones listed throughout the book have inspired you to start your own mindfulness practice and share it with your child. As you work with her to find ways each day to intentionally pay attention to the present moment with kindness, curiosity, and acceptance, you will begin to notice changes—both small and significant—in yourself and your child. You will also get better at recognizing opportunities for new and imaginative ways to create and support mindful moments in your home. If you're not quite sure whether a particular activity is mindful, here are a few things to remember:

- Return to the criteria outlined in chapter 3: does the practice help your child concentrate or get creative, curious, compassionate, or quiet? If so, you're probably on the right track.

- Screens generally don't have a place in mindfulness practice, with the occasional exception of a mindfulness or meditation app (see resources).

- Try to let go of *shoulds* and expectations. Don't worry about the outcome. Mindfulness is about acceptance and kindness, not judgment or perfection.

- Have fun!

We parents race through our days, anticipating problems, making plans, and generally getting through whatever we're doing so we can move on to the next thing. We're always on the go. It's exhausting, it's not sustainable, and if we're not careful, our children will pick up similar habits. Like us, they can end up feeling like their lives are one "Ready, set, go!" after another, without even a moment to calm down, get focused, and reflect on where they've been, where they are, and where they want to go. Fortunately, we can help our children break that cycle. We can teach them how to get ready, get set, and then just breathe. Each time they are able to do that, or each time we can do it with them, we are planting the seeds of mindfulness. We are giving our children skills and practices that will serve them throughout their entire lives.

Acknowledgments

First and foremost, I want to thank all the parents who took time out of their busy schedules to share their wisdom and experiences with me; this book is infinitely stronger as a result of their contributions. In addition, the entire staff at New Harbinger has been amazing throughout this process. Everyone was so supportive and patient with me as I worked to find my voice and perspective for this book. Finally, I want to thank my children and husband. Without them, none of this would be possible; I never would have found my way to mindfulness if I had never become a mother. Without them, I would never have realized just how amazing the present moment can be.

Resources

Here are a number of relevant resources, including picture books for children, books about mindful parenting and mindfulness for adults, guided meditations, and apps for tablets and smartphones. There are many ways to approach mindfulness, and each of the authors listed below has a different voice and style. I encourage you to try a few different options to see what works for you.

Picture Books for Children

There are a number of excellent picture books for children, and more are being published each year. I've listed some favorites on topics such as mindfulness and meditation, compassion, identifying and managing feelings, mindful eating, and yoga, among other things.

Mindfulness and Meditation

Alderfer, Lauren. 2011. *Mindful Monkey, Happy Panda*. Somerville, MA: Wisdom Publications.

DiOrio, Rana. 2010. *What Does It Mean to Be Present?* Belvedere, CA: Little Pickle Press.

MacLean, Kerry Lee. 2004. *Peaceful Piggy Meditation.* Park Ridge, IL: Albert Whitman and Company.

MacLean, Kerry Lee. 2009. *Moody Cow Meditates*. Somerville, MA: Wisdom Publications.

Showers, Paul. 1993. *The Listening Walk*. New York: HarperCollins.

Sister Susan. 2002. *Each Breath a Smile*. Oakland, CA: Plum Blossom Books.

Nhat Hanh, Thich. 2012. *A Handful of Quiet: Happiness in Four Pebbles*. Oakland, CA: Plum Blossom Books.

Roegiers, Maud. 2010. *Take the Time: Mindfulness for Kids*. Washington, DC: Magination Press.

Sosin, Deborah. 2015. *Charlotte and the Quiet Place*. Oakland, CA: Plum Blossom Books.

Compassion and Other Feelings

Kate, Byron. 2009. *Tiger Tiger, Is It True? Four Questions to Make You Smile Again*. Carlsbad, CA: Hay House.

MacLean, Kerry Lee. 2012. *Moody Cow Learns Compassion*. Somerville, MA: Wisdom Publications.

McCloud, Carol. 2006. *Have You Filled a Bucket Today? A Guide to Daily Happiness for Kids*. Northville, MI: Ferne Press.

Hills, Tad. 2009. *Duck & Goose, How Are You Feeling?* New York: Schwartz and Wade.

Silver, Gail. 2009. *Anh's Anger*. Oakland, CA: Plum Blossom Books.

Silver, Gail. 2011. *Steps and Stones: An Anh's Anger Story*. Oakland, CA: Plum Blossom Books.

Silver, Gail. 2014. *Peace, Bugs, and Understanding: An Adventure in Sibling Harmony*. Oakland, CA: Plum Blossom Books.

Rubenstein, Lauren. 2013. *Visiting Feelings*. Washington, DC: Magination Press.

Yoga

Baptiste, Baron. 2012. *My Daddy Is a Pretzel*. Cambridge, MA: Barefoot Books.

Davies, Abbie. 2010. *My First Yoga: Animal Poses*. Mountain View, CA: My First Yoga.

MacLean, Kerry Lee. 2014. *Peaceful Piggy Yoga*. Park Ridge, IL: Albert Whitman and Company.

Miscellaneous: Mindful Eating, Silence, and Your Brain

Deak, JoAnn. 2010. *Your Fantastic Elastic Brain*. Belvedere, CA: Little Pickle Press.

Lemniscates. 2012. *Silence*. Washington, DC: Magination Press.

Marlowe, Sara. 2013. *No Ordinary Apple: A Story About Eating Mindfully*. Somerville, MA: Wisdom Publications.

Miscellaneous: Teaching Mindfulness to Children

Cohen Harper, Jennifer. 2013. *Little Flower Yoga for Kids: A Yoga and Mindfulness Program to Help Your Child Improve Attention and Emotional Balance*. Oakland, CA: New Harbinger Publications.

Hawn, Goldie. 2012. *10 Mindful Minutes: Giving Our Children—and Ourselves—the Social and Emotional Skills to Reduce Stress and Anxiety for Healthier, Happy Lives*. New York: Perigee Books.

Kaiser Greenland, Susan. 2010. *The Mindful Child: How to Help Your Kid Manage Stress and Become Happier, Kinder, and More Compassionate.* New York: Free Press.

Murray, Lorraine. 2012. *Calm Kids: Help Children Relax with Mindful Activities.* Edinburgh: Floris Books.

Nhat Hanh, Thich. 2011. *Planting Seeds: Practicing Mindfulness with Children.* Oakland, CA: Parallax Press.

Saltzman, Amy. 2014. *A Still Quiet Place: A Mindfulness Program for Teaching Children and Adolescents to Ease Stress and Difficult Emotions.* Oakland, CA: New Harbinger Publications.

Snel, Eline. 2013. *Sitting Still Like a Frog: Mindfulness Exercises for Kids (and Their Parents).* Boston: Shambala Publications.

Willard, Christopher. 2011. *Child's Mind: Mindfulness Practices to Help Our Children Be More Focused, Calm, and Relaxed.* Oakland, CA: Parallax Press.

Mindful Parenting

Carter, Christine. 2011. *Raising Happiness: 10 Simple Steps for More Joyful Kids and Happier Parents.* New York: Ballantine Books.

Kabat-Zinn, Myla, and Jon Kabat-Zinn. 1998. *Everyday Blessings: The Inner Work of Mindful Parenting.* New York: Hyperion.

Martin, William. 1999. *The Parent's Tao Te Ching: Ancient Advice for Modern Parents.* Cambridge, MA: Da Capo Press.

McCraith, Sheila. 2014. *Yell Less, Love More: How the Orange Rhino Mom Stopped Yelling at Her Kids—and How You Can Too!* Beverly, MA: Fair Winds Press.

McCurry, Christopher, and Steven Hayes. 2009. *Parenting Your Anxious Child with Mindfulness and Acceptance: A Powerful*

New Approach to Overcoming Fear, Panic, and Worry Using Acceptance and Commitment Therapy. Oakland, CA: New Harbinger Publications.

Miller, Karen Maezen. 2006. *Momma Zen: Walking the Crooked Path of Motherhood*. Boston: Shambhala Publications.

Naumburg, Carla. 2014. *Parenting in the Present Moment: How to Stay Focused on What Really Matters*. Oakland, CA: Parallax Press.

Payne, Kim John, and Lisa Ross. 2010. *Simplicity Parenting: Using the Extraordinary Power of Less to Raise Calmer, Happier, and More Secure Kids*. New York: Ballantine Books.

Race, Kristen. 2014. *Mindful Parenting: Simple and Powerful Solutions for Raising Creative, Engaged, Happy Kids in Today's Hectic World*. New York: St. Martin's Press.

Shapiro, Shauna, and Chris White. 2014. *Mindful Discipline: A Loving Approach to Setting Limits and Raising an Emotionally Intelligent Child*. Oakland, CA: New Harbinger Publications.

Siegel, Daniel, nad Tina Payne Bryson. 2012. *The Whole-Brain Child: 12 Revolutionary Strategies to Nurture Your Child's Developing Mind*. New York: Bantam Books.

Siegel, Daniel, and Mary Hartzell. 2013. *Parenting from the Inside Out: How a Deeper Self-Understanding Can Help You Raise Children Who Thrive*. New York: Penguin Books.

General Mindfulness

Boorstein, Sylvia. 2008. *Happiness Is an Inside Job: Practicing for a Joyful Life*. New York: Ballantine Books.

Germer, Christopher. 2009. *The Mindful Path to Self-Compassion: Freeing Yourself from Destructive Thoughts and Emotions.* New York: Guilford Press.

Harris, Dan. 2014. *10% Happier: How I Tamed the Voice in My Head, Reduced Stress Without Losing My Edge, and Found Self-Help That Actually Works—A True Story.* New York: IT Books.

Kabat-Zinn, Jon. 2013. *Full Catastrophe Living: Using the Wisdom of Your Body and Mind to Face Stress, Pain, and Illness.* Rev. and updated ed. New York: Bantam Books.

Langer, Ellen. 2014. *Mindfulness.* 25th anniversary ed. Boston: Da Capo Press.

Neff, Kristin. 2010. *Self-Compassion: Stop Beating Yourself Up and Leave Insecurity Behind.* New York: William Morrow.

Salzberg, Sharon. 2010. *Real Happiness: The Power of Meditation. A 28-Day Program.* New York: Workman Publishing.

Williams, Mark, and Danny Penman. 2011. *Mindfulness: An Eight-Week Plan for Finding Peace in a Frantic World.* New York: Rodale Books.

Books to Help You Simplify and Declutter Your Home

Becker, Joshua. 2014. *Clutterfree with Kids: Change Your Thinking. Discover New Habits. Free Your Home.* Peoria, AZ: Becoming Minimalist Press.

Green, Melva, and Lauren Rosenfeld. 2014. *Breathing Room: Open Your Heart by Decluttering Your Home.* New York: Atria Books.

Jay, Francine. 2010. *The Joy of Less, A Minimalist Living Guide: How to Declutter, Organize, and Simplify Your Life*. Medford, NJ: Anja Press.

Kondo, Marie. 2014. *The Life-Changing Magic of Tidying Up: The Japanese Art of Decluttering and Organizing*. Berkeley, CA: Ten Speed Press.

Guided Meditations

Clarke, Carolyn. 2012. *Imaginations: Fun Relaxation Stories and Meditations for Kids* (Volume 1). Charleston: CreateSpace.

Clarke, Carolyn. 2014. *Imaginations: Fun Relaxation Stories and Meditations for Kids* (Volume 2). San Diego, CA: Bambino Yoga.

Kerr, Christiane. 2005. *Enchanted Meditations for Kids*. Borough Green, Kent, UK: Diviniti Publishing. Audiobook and compact disc.

Kerr, Christiane. 2005. *Bedtime Meditations for Kids*. Borough Green, Kent, UK: Diviniti Publishing. Audiobook and compact disc.

Kerr, Christiane. 2007. *Mermaids and Fairy Dust: Magical Meditations for Girls of All Ages*. Borough Green, Kent, UK: Diviniti Publishing. Audiobook and compact disc.

Kluge, Nicola. 2014. *Mindfulness for Kids I: 7 Children's Meditations & Mindfulness Practices to Help Kids Be More Focused, Calm, and Relaxed*. Houston: Arts and Education Foundation. Book and compact disc.

Kluge, Nicola. 2014. *Mindfulness for Kids II: 7 Children's Stories & Mindfulness Practices to Help Kids Be More Focused, Calm, and Relaxed.* Houston: Arts and Education Foundation. Compact disc.

Pincus, Donna. 2012. *I Can Relax! A Relaxation CD for Children.* Boston: The Child Anxiety Network. Compact disc.

Roberton-Jones, Michelle. 2013. *Bedtime: Guided Meditations for Children.* Tring, UK: Paradise Music. Audiobook and compact disc.

Saltzman, Amy. 2007. *Still Quiet Place: Mindfulness for Young Children.* Portland: CD Baby. Compact disc.

Sukhu, Chitra. 2002. *Guided Meditation for Children—Journey into the Elements.* Playa Del Ray, CA: New Age Kids. Compact disc.

Apps

Buddhify. This app includes over eighty guided meditations of different lengths and for a variety of situations. Most appropriate for adults. $4.99 on iTunes, $2.99 on Google Play.

Calm.com. Website and app with guided meditations for adults; appropriate for children as well. Free on iTunes and Google Play.

Enchanted Meditation for Kids 1, by Christiane Kerr. This app includes guided meditations such as "Jellyfish Relaxation" and "The Magic Rainbow" for children ages three to nine. $2.99 on iTunes, $3.36 on Google Play.

Headspace. Includes a variety of "meditation packs" of different lengths and themes. Most appropriate for adults. Ten guided meditations are free on iTunes and Google Play; additional meditations available for a fee.

Insight Timer. Meditation timer and guided meditations for adults. Free on iTunes and Google Play.

iZen Garden. This app transforms your smartphone screen into a portable Zen garden. Use your fingers to trace the sand or move the stones as you design your garden. $3.99 on iTunes and Google Play.

Meditate Now Kids, by Hansen Stin. Includes five guided meditations for kids: feel better, calm down, take a magical vacation, go on an adventure, and fall asleep. $1.99 on iTunes.

Meditation—Tibetan Bowls, by RockCat Studio Limited. Choose a singing bowl and tap it to hear the sound. Appropriate for children and adults. Free on iTunes and Google Play.

My *First Yoga—Animal Poses for Kids*, by the Atom Group. This app leads children through a variety of easy animal yoga poses. Companion to the book of the same name, by Abbie Davies. Free on iTunes.

Smiling Mind. Guided meditations for children and adolescents, ages seven and up. Free to try on iTunes and Google Play.

ZenFriend. Meditation timer and tracker with guided meditations. Free on iTunes, upgrades available.

References

Ames, C., J. Richardson, S. Payne, P. Smith, and E. Leigh. 2014. “Mindfulness-Based Cognitive Therapy for Depression in Adolescents.” *Child and Adolescent Mental Health* 19 (1): 74–78.

Beach, S. R. 2014. “40 Ways to Bring Mindfulness to Your Days.” *Left Brain Buddha* (blog), April 21. http://leftbrainbuddha.com/40-ways-bring-mindfulness-days/.

Bei, B., M. L. Byrne, C. Ivens, J. Waloszek, M. J. Woods, P. Dudgeon, G. Murray, C. L. Nicholas, J. Trinder, and N. B. Allen. 2013. “Pilot Study of a Mindfulness-Based, Multi-Component, In-School Group Sleep Intervention in Adolescent Girls.” *Early Intervention in Psychiatry* 7 (2): 213–20.

Black, D., and R. Fernando. 2014. “Mindfulness Training and Classroom Behavior Among Lower-Income and Ethnic Minority Elementary School Children.” *Journal of Child and Family Studies* 23 (7): 1242–46.

Borchard, T. 2013. “Sanity Break: How Does Mindfulness Reduce Depression? An Interview with John Teasdale, PhD.” *Everyday Health*, November 11. http://www.everydayhealth.com/columns/therese-borchard-sanity-break/how-does-mindfulness-reduce-depression-an-interview-with-john-teasdale-ph-d/.

Brown, P. L. 2007. “In the Classroom, a New Focus on Quieting the Mind.” *New York Times*, June 16. http://www.nytimes.com/2007/06/16/us/16mindful.html.

Centers for Disease Control and Regulation. 2014. "Attention-Deficit/Hyperactivity Disorder: Data and Statistics." http://www.cdc.gov/ncbddd/adhd/data.html/.

Chai, P. 2012. "Natural Born Chillers." *Daily Life*, February 13. http://www.dailylife.com.au/life-and-love/parenting-and-families/natural-born-chillers-20120213-1qx87.html/.

Cohen Harper, J. 2013. *Little Flower Yoga for Kids: A Yoga and Mindfulness Program to Help Your Child Improve Attention and Emotional Balance.* Oakland, CA: New Harbinger Publications.

Flook, L., S. L. Smalley, M. J. Kitil, B. M. Galla, S. Kaiser Greenland, J. Locke, E. Ishijima, and C. Kasari. 2010. "Effects of Mindful Awareness Practices on Executive Functions in Elementary School Children." *Journal of Applied School Psychology* 26 (1): 70–95.

Hölzel, B., S. W. Lazar, T. Gard, Z. Schuman-Olivier, D. R. Vago, and U. Ott. 2011. "How Does Mindfulness Meditation Work? Proposing Mechanisms of Action from a Conceptual and Neural Perspective." *Perspectives on Psychological Science* 6 (6): 537–59.

Kailus, J. 2014. "How to Become a Mindful Parent: An Interview with Jon and Myla Kabat Zinn, authors of *Everyday Blessings: The Inner Work of Mindful Parenting.*" *Gaiam Life*. http://life.gaiam.com/article/how-become-mindful-parent/.

Kaiser Greenland, S. 2010. *The Mindful Child: How to Help Your Kid Manage Stress and Become Happier, Kinder, and More Compassionate.* New York: Free Press.

Kuyken, W., K. Weare, O. C. Ukoumunne, R. Vicary, N. Motton, R. Burnett, C. Cullen, S. Hennelly, and F. Huppert. 2013. "Effectiveness of the Mindfulness in Schools Programme: Non-Randomised Controlled Feasibility Study." *The British Journal of Psychiatry* 203 (2): 126–31.

Lazarus, R. 1966. *Psychological Stress and the Coping Mechanism*. New York: McGraw-Hill.

MacLean, K. L. 2009. *Moody Cow Meditates*. Somerville, MA: Wisdom Publications.

McCloud, C. 2006. *Have You Filled a Bucket Today? A Guide to Daily Happiness for Kids*. Northville, MI: Ferne Press.

Mendelson, T., M. T. Greenberg, J. K. Dariotis, L. F. Gould, B. L. Rhoades, and P. J. Leaf. 2010. "Feasibility and Preliminary Outcomes of a School-Based Mindfulness Intervention for Urban Youth." *Journal of Abnormal Child Psychology* 38 (7): 985–94.

Miller, K. M. 2009. "How to Meditate." *Cheerio Road* (blog), July 11. http://karenmaezenmiller.com/how-to-meditate/.

Nhat Hanh, T. 2011. *Planting Seeds: Practicing Mindfulness with Children*. Berkeley, CA: Parallax Press.

Payne, K. J., and L. Ross. 2010. *Simplicity Parenting: Using the Extraordinary Power of Less to Raise Calmer, Happier, and More Secure Kids*. New York: Ballantine Books.

Razza, R., D. Bergen-Cico, and K. Raymond. 2015. "Enhancing Preschoolers' Self-Regulation via Mindful Yoga." *Journal of Child and Family Studies* 24 (2): 372–85.

Saltzman, A. 2014. *A Still Quiet Place: A Mindfulness Program for Teaching Children and Adolescents to Ease Stress and Difficult Emotions*. Oakland, CA: New Harbinger Publications.

Salvucci, D., and N. Taatgen. 2010. *The Multitasking Mind*. New York: Oxford University Press.

Salzberg, S. 2010. *Real Happiness: The Power of Meditation*. New York: Workman Publishing.

Srinivasan, M. 2014. *Teach, Breathe, Learn: Mindfulness in and out of the Classroom*. Oakland, CA: Parallax Press.

Tan, L., and G. Martin. 2015. "Taming the Adolescent Mind: A Randomised Controlled Trial Examining Clinical Efficacy of an Adolescent Mindfulness-Based Group Programme." *Child and Adolescent Mental Health* 20 (1): 49–55.

Tippett, K. 2009. "God Has a Sense of Humor, Too." Radio interview with Jon Kabat-Zinn on *On Being*, April 16. http://www.onbeing.org/program/opening-our-lives/138/.

Willard, C. 2010. *Child's Mind: Mindfulness Practices to Help Our Children Be More Focused, Calm, and Relaxed*. Oakland, CA: Parallax Press.

Willems, M. 2003. *Don't Let the Pigeon Drive the Bus*. New York: Hyperion.

Parent Contributors

I would like to express my deepest gratitude to the following parents, who are committed to practicing and teaching mindfulness and compassion with their own families. This book exists because they were kind and generous enough to share their wisdom, knowledge, and experience with me.

Allison Andrews, PsyD, clinical psychologist. http://www.allisonandrewspsyd.com/

Rita Arens, author of the young adult novel *The Obvious Game.* http://www.blogher.com/myprofile/rita-arens/

Jessica Berger Gross, writer and yogi, author of *Estranged* and *Enlightened: How I Lost 40 Pounds with a Yoga Mat, Fresh Pineapple, and a Beagle Pointer.* http://www.jessicabergergross.com/

Janah Boccio, LCSW, clinical social worker

Nicole Churchill, MA, MT-BC, licensed music therapist and co-founder of Samadhi Integral. http://www.samadhiintegral.com/

Jennifer Cohen Harper, founder of Little Flower Yoga and author of *Little Flower Yoga for Kids: A Yoga and Mindfulness Program to Help Your Child Improve Attention and Emotional Balance.* http://www.littlefloweryoga.com/

Estelle Erasmus, journalist, author, and former magazine editor. http://www.musingsonmotherhoodmidlife.com/

Nanci Ginty Butler, LICSW, clinical social worker

April Hadley, MSW, cofounder of the Grand Rapids Center for Mindfulness. http://grandrapidscenterformindfulness.com/

Danya Handelsman, pediatric physical therapist and parent coach. http://www.danyaparentcoach.org/

Gina Hassan, PhD, mindfulness teacher and psychologist http://www.ginahassan.com/

Joshua Herzig-Marx, my husband

Dara James, MS, mindful eating expert

Ellie Klein, owner of Family Restorative Yoga http://www.familyrestore.com/

Brian Leaf, MA, author of *Misadventures of a Parenting Yogi.* http://www.misadventures-of-a-yogi.com/

Josh Lobel, father of three and dedicated mindfulness practitioner

Alison Auderieth Lobron, MEd, early childhood educator and writer. http://frootloopsblog.wordpress.com/

Nina Manolson, MA, CHC, holistic health coach and psychology-of-eating coach, founder of the Nourished Woman Nation. http://www.ninamanolson.com/

Sheila McCraith, author of *Yell Less, Love More: How the Orange Rhino Mom Stopped Yelling at Her Kids—And How You Can Too!* http://theorangerhino.com/

Lisa A. McCrohan, LCSW-C, RYT, psychotherapist, compassion coach, and poet. http://www.barefootbarn.com/

Lindsey Mead, writer. http://www.adesignsovast.com/

Josh Misner, PhD, author of the Mindful Dad blog. http://mindfuldad.org/

Meghan Nathanson, writer and artist. http://www.meghannathanson.com/

Sheila Pai, parent coach and founder of A Living Family. http://www.sheilapai.com/

Miranda Phillips, teacher and community organizer

Sarah Rudell Beach, MEd, executive director of Brilliant Mindfulness, mindfulness instructor, and author of the blog *Left Brain Buddha*. http://www.brilliantmindfulness.com/

Rabbi Danya Ruttenberg, author of *Nurturing the Wow: Parenting as a Spiritual Practice* and *Surprised by God: How I Learned to Stop Worrying and Love Religion*. http://danyaruttenberg.net/

Sara Schairer, founder of Compassion It. http://www.compassionit.com/

Nicole Snyder, cofounder of Inspired Family. http://inspiredfamily.us/

Erica Streit-Kaplan, MSW, MPH, social worker and public health professional

Susan Whitman, PA-C, integrative health coach and founder of Trail to Wellness. http://www.trailtowellness.com/

Carla Naumburg, PhD, is a clinical social worker, writer, and mother. Her first book, *Parenting in the Present Moment*, was published by Parallax Press in 2014. Naumburg is the Mindful Parenting blogger for psychcentral.com, and a contributing editor at kveller.com. Her writing has appeared in *The New York Times*, *The Washington Post*, and *The Huffington Post*, as well as in a number of academic journals and online magazines. Naumburg holds an MSW and a PhD in social work, and she has an advanced certificate in mindfulness and psychotherapy. She currently lives outside of Boston, MA, with her husband and two young daughters. Connect with Carla and read all of her writing at www.carlanaumburg.com.